PROTO-TOOLS 1
TRANSCRIPTION
16-17 NOVEMBER 2013
FLAT TIME HOUSE

ANTONIA BLOCKER, NEIL CHAPMAN, PETER FILLINGHAM, VERINA GFADER, JULIKA GITTNER, MARK HARRIS, JONATHAN KEMP, STEPHEN KNOTT, COLM LALLY (Ed.), JOHN LATHAM, PETER LEWIS, GIBSON/ MARTELLI, FAY NICOLSON, ANDRÉS MONTENEGRO ROSERO, ALEX SCHADY, REHANA ZAMAN

E:vent

INTRODUCTION

Proto-tools considers the role of the tool within artistic practice, both as a means to create material effect and as a device to progress a way of thinking. Locating the point of energy of the artwork not at the moment of its encounter with an audience, or indeed the market, but rather at the site of production, Proto-tools interrogates the interaction between the artist and the object in production. In what ways do the often 'proflexive' (or unknowing) activities involved in making inform reflexive understanding in the work of the artist? How far can we extend the definition of a tool? Is it naïve to imagine that altering the original use-function of the tools of production can push against the market logic of efficiency, and thereby open up an alternative engagement with the world?

Within the context of Flat Time House, Proto-tools manifests as a display of works in the room known as 'the Mind'. Here selected works by Jonathan Kemp, Colm Lally and Fay Nicolson interact with the permanent installation of works by John Latham. While in 'the Hand' space of the house, the site of production, a series of presentations and conversations takes place in an essayic attempt to further evolve the concerns of the project.

Proto-tools symposium panelists include Peter Fillingham (with Peter Lewis), Verina Gfader, Mark Harris, Andrés Montenegro Rosero and Alex Schady; chaired by Antonia Blocker.

Artist Conversations include discussions between Neil Chapman, Julika Gittner, Colm Lally, Gibson/Martelli, Fay Nicolson and Rehana Zaman; with an introduction by Stephen Knott.

TRANSCRIPTION NOTES

This document is a transcription of the Proto-tools event at Flat Time House. The document contains verbatim transcriptions of the discussions and presentations that took place. Also contained in the document is a number of texts submitted after the event. These include submissions by Verina Gfader, Mark Harris, Stephen Knott and Andrés Montenegro Rosero, all of which are texts or notes that were read from or used as the basis of their presentation at the Proto-tools event.

The verbatim transcriptions are divided into two columns, speaker and text. The speaker column indicates the source of the communication and the text column contains the transcription of the communication. In the text, one dash (–) is used to indicate a speaker's pause or a self-interruption. Two dashes (– –) are used to indicate an interruption by another speaker or other abrupt stop in communication.

Speakers are identified as follows:

AB	Antonia Blocker
NC	Neil Chapman
RG	Ruth Gibson (from Gibson/Martelli)
PF	Peter Fillingham
VG	Verina Gfader
JG	Julika Gittner
MH	Mark Harris
JK	Jonathan Kemp
SK	Stephen Knott
CL	Colm Lally
BM	Bruno Martelli (from Gibson/Martelli)
FN	Fay Nicolson
AMR	Andrés Montenegro Rosero
AS	Alex Schady
RZ	Rehana Zaman
AM	Audience member

DAY 1
PROTO-TOOLS
SYMPOSIUM

SUBMITTED TEXT

SOMETIMES DOING IS UNDOING AND SOMETIMES UNDOING IS DOING
ANDRÉS MONTENEGRO ROSERO

In 1990, the Belgian artist Francis Alÿs (b. Antwerp, 1959) produced *Placing pillows*. Created soon after his relocation to Mexico City, and in the aftermath of the 1985 earthquake, *Placing pillows* was a walk, a stroll, in which the artist placed pillows in broken window frames around Mexico City's historic centre. Alÿs's "subtle gesture of symbolic healing," as described by Cuauhtémoc Medina, was his earliest attempt at developing a "methodology of walking [as] a means to physically inscribe narratives into the city fabric" [Francis Alÿs and Cuauhtémoc Medina, "Entries," in *Francis Alÿs: A Story of Deception,* (2010)]. Through *Placing pillows,* Alÿs attempted to insert a story into the memory of the city by allegorically 'repairing' some of the broken windows with unexpected objects, the pillows. These, for Medina, "infused dream-like passages into daily life." The work symbolically addressed a turbulent reality; it was an attempt to 'mend' the wounds left by the natural disaster, which implied a process of careful observation of said reality. It also narrativised the urban fabric by directly including it as a protagonist of a series of 'repairs,' similar to a dream-like fairy-tale. Furthermore, and perhaps more importantly, *Placing pillows* was Alÿs's earliest attempt at creating a "sculptural situation" out of a simple stroll.

Placing pillows emphasised the action itself – Alÿs's actual insertion of the pillows into the physical material of Mexico City. Through their physical positioning, the pillows acted as a trace of Alÿs's symbolic act of mending, while at the same time, plotted an alternative cartography of the city that focused on the incomplete, the fragmentary, broken, the unbuilt, the un-mended. Because the action can be described in a concise sentence, "While walking around the centre of Mexico City, I place pillows in the frames of broken windows," Alÿs's stroll had the potential to be easily circulated through rumours and, therefore, add a narrative layer to the existing architecture without physically adding to it.

Dissolving sculpture

In the catalogue for Alÿs's 2010 Irish Museum of Modern Art painting exhibition, *Les temps du sommeil,* he described the work *Seven lives of garbage*

(1995) as follows, "On the night of 4 February 1994, I put 7 identical bronze sculptures painted 7 distinct colours in 7 plastic bags and I dropped them on garbage piles in 7 districts of Mexico City. On the following days, months, years, I have wandered through local flea markets looking for the missing sculptures to resurface. As for now I have found 2 out of 7" [*Francis Alÿs: Le temps du sommeil* (2010)]. As his account suggests, the work emphasised the circulation of the sculptural objects rather than the objects themselves; the sculptures were only the excuse for making visible a complex informal circuit of exchange characteristic of several megalopolises – trash scavenging. As the title of the work suggests, discarded objects have more than one life – they are appropriated and reused (re-sold in this case), moving "through different social strata," as Medina noted, in this case from artist's studio, to garbage bin, to flea market. Mutating roles and values, the re-found bronze snail echoes the multivalent indexical associations of the pillows of *Placing pillows*. Both pillows and the re-found sculptures simultaneously act as objects within a plot – pillows placed, snails dumped – while simultaneously mapping out different systems of circulation – the pillows as markers of symbolic urban healing and the snails as 'probes' of parallel economic systems. For *Seven lives of garbage,* Alÿs released a series of objects into the world of garbage in Mexico City which, upon re-discovery in a flea market, acted as bearers of a series of transactions and transitions – both economic and symbolic – of their own paseo. The re-found snail, plucked away from the circuit of re-use, is not the same bronze snail that was released by Alÿs; it has been fundamentally altered by virtue of its circulation in different realms.

If *Seven lives of garbage* dissolved the single sculptural object (multiple snails which suggest multiple routes through which each of the seven can traverse and therefore bring to light) into a discursive field, *Paradox of praxis 1 (sometimes doing something leads to nothing)* 1997, literally melted a perfect minimalist form. It was described by Medina as "a literalist dematerialisation of the art object that took place from 9:15am to 6:47pm on a mild day in Mexico City" [*Recent Political forms: Radical Pursuits in Mexico. Santiago Sierra, Francis Alÿs, Minerva Cuevas,* (2000)]. As he commented, for *Paradox of praxis 1,* the artist "pushed an ice block through the streets of Mexico City until it completely melted away, as if eroded by the urban surroundings." The documentation of the action, a five minute documentary video or a series of photographs of the artist pushing the block, shows the gradual dissolution of the block while highlighting the physical strain implied in such action. We see, for example, how difficult it is to move the block at the beginning of the 'walk', we see the artist bent over, leaning and pushing against the block with great difficulty. As the day passes, and as the cube becomes smaller, it becomes lighter; enough to be kicked around through the streets. The video ends with an image of a small puddle of water surrounded by curious kids, documenting the complete disappearance of the former object. The work did not produce any final result besides its own unfolding (and documentation); in the end the ice melted. By having no visible or direct material product, *Paradox of praxis 1* was an investigation into the dynamics of production or of the logic of effort vs. results. After all, its subtitle is *sometimes doing something leads to nothing,* a statement aimed at what Alÿs considered the understanding of sculpture at the time, "as a permanent material construction" [*Entries*]. For *Paradox of praxis 1,* Alÿs directly countered this notion and advanced an artistic language that, as observed by Betti-Sue Hertz, "opened the object of sculpture to the urban environs" ["The Circumstance Is Mexico: Art Practice for the Transitory Cosmopole," in *Axis Mexico: Common objects and Cosmopolitan Actions,* (2002)]. The pristine cube of ice, reminiscent of a polished minimalist sculpture, was made to interact with the city and as a result it completely disappeared. As a critique of an artistic definition – sculpture as a material construction – it underlined the inoperativity of such conceptualisations when displaced onto the urban context of Mexico City. As Medina argued, "Seen in the context of the history of sculpture, the work might be taken as a parable of the 'thaw' of the Minimalist object, as if a Sol LeWitt or Tony Smith work were consumed by the complex phenomenology of the social resistance of the megalopolis" [*Recent Political forms: Radical Pursuits in Mexico. Santiago Sierra, Francis Alÿs, Minerva Cuevas*].

Both *Seven lives of garbage* and *Paradox of praxis 1* emphasise the dissolution of the sculptural object – one through circulation and the other through literal dematerialisation. *Seven lives of garbage* focused on the act of insertion into parallel systems, highlighting both the initial act of release of the sculptures but also the different social strata through which the snails traversed in order to be re-found and purchased by the artist. Although the bronze objects effectively catalysed a series of reactions, the emphasis of the action was on the atomisation of that sculptural object into different registers and the spaces that it traversed; in other words, the trajectories plotted by its actual, physical circulation. Similarly, albeit perhaps more effectively doing away with the sculptural object, *Paradox of praxis 1* enacted a physical disintegration of the ice cube through its circulation. Both works call into question the materiality of sculpture by, as Medina argued, displacing "the sculptural values from objects to situations and agents."

But *Seven lives of garbage* and *Paradox of praxis 1* share another, perhaps more important, affinity. If, as argued so far, the bronze snails of *Seven lives of garbage* are relevant as probes that mapped what Alÿs and Medina called "the underground economies on which the metabolism of a whole society in the so-called Third World relies," [*Entries*] – and therefore provided a fragmentary glimpse of these circuits – *Paradox of praxis 1,* also provided fleeting glimpses into the urban context of Mexico City's historic centre. Alÿs is not pushing an ice block in his studio or a pristine gallery space. As Medina noted, the action "provided an oblique glimpse into city life, which continued on, oblivious to the epic quality of Alÿs's performance" [*Recent Political forms: Radical Pursuits in Mexico. Santiago Sierra, Francis Alÿs, Minerva Cuevas*]. As both photographs and video show, Alÿs's action passed mostly unnoticed; only at the end do a few kids gather around the last remains of the ice cube; there are no suggestions that he was offered help or that anyone disrupted his stroll. In this way, *Paradox of praxis 1* is also a chronicle that provides a glimpse into the behaviour of the city, the reaction or lack of reaction of its citizens, how they conduct themselves in public space. At the same time, and just like *Seven lives of garbage* was an exploration of underground economic spaces, *Paradox of praxis 1* also offers a series of views into the physical conditions of the city, its building and urban structures; the colours of façades, the consistency of the pavement; the dirt, the sun, the traffic. As a clear rejection of the physicality of sculpture, *Paradox of praxis 1* not only literally dissolved the sculptural object but also used it as an excuse for a photographic view of the daily life of Mexico City. Doubly de-emphasising the physicality of sculpture, the work proposes instead a mobile practice articulated at the crossroads between social encounters and sculptural situations [*Entries*].

SUBMITTED TEXT

NOTEBOOKS SPIRIT
VERINA GFADER

A first plan for today was to put forward a theoretical proposition through which to approach the substantial work of the sociologist and political philosopher Antonio Negri. In particular, by proposing the format and practice of interviewing as a place to think and enact the "common," a fundamental term within Negri's work (and that of [Michael] Hardt and Negri), I wanted to investigate a number of issues around the constitution of places for exchange, mediation, affect and negotiation – a sort of open knowledge production.

Instead of drifting however into this conceptual–abstract space, my presentation follows an intellectual storytelling à la Irit Rogoff, and Negri and Hardt's "common" as a means and device, resulting in a short diary, which takes account of my encounter with Negri in June 2012. What became apparent while working on 'interview modes' is, as I would like to suggest, an ambiguous relationship to material as well as immaterial production. The more than two hours conversation with Negri became a space for exchanging ideas and histories or the lack thereof, but more importantly, it also became a reality of enacting knowledge and non-knowledge, thereby affirming an anticipatory element in the very act of verbal exchange. Conceptually, the process of interviewing then can be seen as a projection of or into the future, the yet-to-come; precisely and especially because interviewing also necessarily retrieves the 'past' aiming to recover something yet unspoken or unpublished. Interviewing works with memory and intuition as a fundamental tool. Interviewing, to a degree, insists on enacting deformations of histories that necessarily take place in this 'set-up' in between formal and informal. Particularly when conducted in a foreign language, with a translator or interpreter negotiating and intervening in what's being said and discussed, or left out. One important question remains, how to enact the production of knowledge/non-knowledge without knowledge becoming a commodity.

Diary: In May 2012 Negri agreed to be interviewed for EP1, a book edited by Alex Coles and Catharine Rossi on the Italian avant-garde 1968–76 published by Sternberg Press, Berlin, May 2013. The volume focuses on the radical interdisciplinary impulse of the period across art, architecture and design. On paper, I am involved in this particular volume as an editorial manager and contributor, and in the book series EP (founded and directed by Alex) as the creative director; what that means is a plural role – artistic, curatorial, conceptual, managerial and editorial etc. A residency at Sternberg Press in January 2013 supported this multiple engagement.

Curatorially-conceptually, when discussing the contribution to EP1 by a theoretician of that time, I suggested Negri among other writers, thinkers and activists from the Autonomist movement, the most innovative post-'68 radical movement in the West. Negri's work was familiar to me mostly through his writings with Hardt on

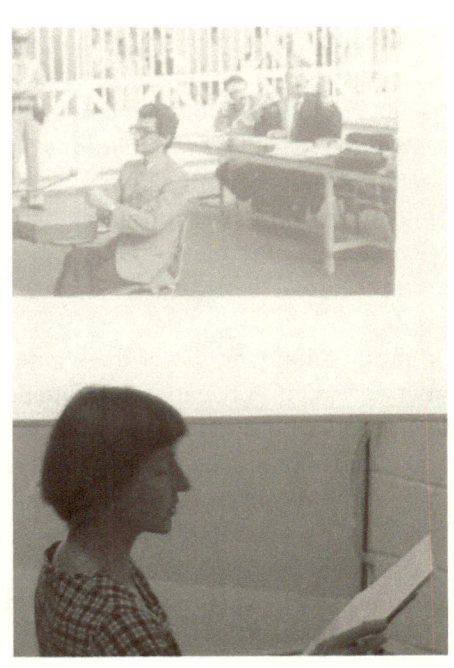

VERINA GFADER

immaterial labor, multitude and self-organised forms of resistance, but in a way I always felt more drawn to his writings as a single author, especially *Time for Revolution* (English translation: Continuum, 2003; Originally published: *La constituzione del tempo,* Manifestolibri, 1997). At this moment – with a very specific enquiry in mind, Italy in the mid 1960s – my focus shifted discreetly, yet significantly towards Negri's years as an academic and political activist before he was accused in the late 1970s of various charges including being the mastermind of the left-wing terrorist group Red Brigades (*Brigate Rosse* or BR), involved in the May 1978 assassination of Aldo Moro, two-time Prime Minister of Italy, and leader of the Christian-Democrat Party, among others. He fled to France and returned to Italy in 1997 after 14 years in exile.

After inviting him to contribute to EP1, he agreed to an interview in Venice in June. He asked for conducting the interview either in Italian or French and to send the written questions at least one week before the meeting. The drafting of these questions required more general but also very specific research into Negri's persona, work, the various involvements – keeping in mind the context of EP1. For us one focus, besides Italy in the 1960s (workers movements, economic crisis, cultural shifts), was to emphasise both the optic of the present, and the role of theory and activism in relation to the transforming sociopolitical landscape. More particularly, one of the issue we wanted to explore with him was his response to the art, architecture and design produced in this moment, that he may have been in tension with. This is the context of a flourishing Italian cinema, Arte Povera (including Michelangelo Pistoletto, Giuseppe Penone), and the so-called radical architecture collectives, Archizoom, Superstudio, Gruppo Strum or 9999.

From an initial long list of questions with themes such as Theory Factory, Abstraction, or Publication formats and circulation, it became clear that my focus would be on text/theory/workers movement (*operaism* = workerism) and creative practices. For example: A. What status did text and theory have in relation to forming groups and alliances? B. Was the involvement in the academy and academic matters for you without conflicts? (Theoretical rigour of Operaists versus intellectual creativity of Autonomia and academia more generally.) What were the conflicts? The institution as a workers' project?

This reduction led into further reading, including Italian language books. I rediscovered, for instance, the seminal book *The Project of Autonomy* (Princeton Architectural Press, 2008) by architect and theoretician Pier Vittorio Aureli. The sections on the primacy of theory in architectural practice, more specifically, proposing architecture – theory – as urban reinvention without planning (an 'action,' a kernel of 'revolution'), and the relation to professional practice and labour relations are quite interesting with respect to the current transdisciplinary practices and a certain lack of pure theory. To me, what hasn't been resolved in the conversation with Negri, which was also one of the preliminary points of attention, is the question if there hasn't been a conflict between his political engagement and Antonio's academic position.

Projected images: Negri, *Potere Operaio* (Workers' Power)

Images from Sylvère Lotringer and Christian Marazzi (eds) *Autonomia: Post-Political Politics*. Semiotext(e), 1980.

And the comic strip of the Aldo Moro kidnapping by the Red Brigades which was published in the first issue of Metropoli (weekly feature on multi-cultural Italy in *La Repubblica,* Italian daily newspaper).

Practicalities: A translator from Trieste, Valentina Milan, confirmed her participation in the project. Liaising with her was essential for the actual conversation with Negri. In anticipation of the meeting and theoretical debate, she asked for relevant readings and links which would help her to negotiate the ideas exchanged between Negri and myself during the communication. Valentina became indispensible in the conversation and post-production as an intermediary, interface and collaborator.

Action Material: The interview in Negri's apartment in Venice lasted 2,5 hours. Initially the conversation developed along the written questions but soon proliferated into various ideas and new links. At the same time two enquiries or topics crystallised clearly, the "magazine movement" and Negri's crucial, partially ambivalent, involvement in it; and his to a degree conflictual relation to art.

Slides: journal covers (reference: Aureli, *The Project of Autonomy*)

Contropiano 2, 1971: Founded by Alberto Asor Rosa, Massimo Cacciari, and Antonio Negri in 1968 and published until 1971. Negri left the journal after the first issue. Unlike *Classe operaia,* its focus was more on theory than intervention.

Quaderni rossi 2, 1962: Journal founded by Raniero Panzieri in 1961. It ran for 6 issues, ceasing publication in 1965. Its central themes were the capitalist organisation of work and the possibility of workers' autonomy.

Classe operaia 1 and 3, 1964: Founded by Mario Tronti in 1964 as a monthly journal dedicated to the cause of "struggling workers," *Classe operaia* was produced by Operaists who split off from the Quaderni Rossi group at the end of 1963. The last issue appeared in 1966. The two approaches of the journal were exemplified by editorials published in two of the early issues: Tronti's seminal "manifesto" "Lenin in Inghilterra" called for a Leninist use of the party organisation within advanced capitalist society; and Antonio Negri's "Operai senza alleati" argued for self-organised forms of struggle.

Course booklets prepared at IUAV (Istituto Universitario di Architettura di Venezia, Institute of Architecture Venice) and published by Cluva, 1965: During the academic years 1963-64 and 1964-65, Rossi joined Carlo Aymonino as assistant professor in Aymonio's newly established program at the IUAV, "Organizational Characteristics of Buildings." Prior to this, Rossi had carried out research on Milanese residential typologies. In their collaboration, Rossi and Aymonino further developed the typological analysis of the city that Rossi had initiated, building up the theoretical premises of what later would become one of the main themes of the "Scuola di Venezia": the relationship between the city's visible and material form (morphology) and its inner structure (typology). The two seminal course booklets published at the conclusion of each course in 1963 and 1964, on aspects and problems of building typology and the format of the concept of building typology respectively, exemplify the method applied by Aymonino and Rossi, which was to prepare their classes by writing theoretical and methodological essays.

Arte Futurista. Reprint of a comic strip in the seventh issue of the Operaist journal *Classe operaia,* 1964. It originally appeared in Pioniere dell'Unità, a supplement to the Communist Party newspaper *L'Unità.* It was reprinted with the caption "Futurist Art – the Communist perspective," and exemplifies the techno-utopianism of the institutional Left, which envisioned new technology as engendering an Eden of work.

Returning to the interview: Post-production included transcribing and translating, editing, negotiating various points with Negri, confirming final edit, identifying the right place in EP1. On another interesting, less mechanical and technical level, it involved thinking about corrections, pauses, modes of cutting, extracting, reformulating. A further level, to me the most fascinating, is in what way the 'event' demands further research and how it affects your other work and activities more generally, on both a micro – and macroscopic level.

In conclusion, to me, the interview is a medium of time. Its relation to knowledge and knowledge production is fundamentally based on the production of subjectivities, and a state and process of being in common. The conversation with Negri results in the material itself, actual material, print, which at the same time means enquiry ... Being situated in a particular context, in this case the book EP1, the interview – its text – affects and modifies this very context. As a method or methodology the interview's value lies in how it organises and 'tools' new social relations. It's unpredictability, and the faults and errors that come with it, is a shared writing, un-and re-writing of such relations. The Negri interview – and in certain ways the "magazine movement" described by him – manifests and affirms the process of constituting this.

SUBMITTED TEXT

CINEMA, STUDIO, TOOLS
MARK HARRIS

We are used to thinking of artworks being shadowed by copies, or being copies themselves – Sherrie Levine, Jeff Koons, Alan McCollum and others in the 1980s, influenced by Baudrillard, conspicuously initiated this process under the concept of appropriation. But what if for every artwork there were thousands, or millions, of versions, each of which slightly altered some aspect of its counterparts to the point where no original existed other than the one we were working on, the same however, going for every other artist working on their versions? Certainly Mike Bidlo, Richard Pettibone and Elaine Sturtevant have been engaged in versions of this act for a long time, but I am imagining something with overwhelming reach. What if each of those millions of alternates itself had its thousands of additional versions representing its changing physical condition across the span of centuries? This is not far from Jorge Luis Borges's vision in the well-known short story *Library of Babel* where "every copy is unique, irreplaceable, but (since the Library is total) there are always several hundred thousand imperfect facsimiles: works which differ only in a letter or a comma". Borges' story owed its central idea to anarchist ringleader Louis-August Blanqui's *Eternity by the Stars: an astronomical hypothesis,* which he wrote in prison in 1871 towards the end of a life of continuous revolutionary activism.

"Any celestial body, whatever it is, exists in infinite numbers in time and space, not only under one of its aspects, but such that it appears at every second of its life span, from its birth till its death. Every being great or small, live or inert, that is spread over its surface, shares the privilege of this immortality...Yet there is one shortcoming: there is no progress. Alas! No, these are vulgar reissues, repetitions. So too are the copies of past worlds, so too are those of future worlds...Let us not forget that everything we could have been on this earth, we are it somewhere else".

Walter Benjamin read despair in this speculation on account of Blanqui's failure to effect radical political change through insurrection. He also recognised here an antinomy of progress which through the reign of commodities promotes middle class economic prosperity as a sign of advancement while creating a deprived proletarian class for whom that economic indicator only becomes a further incentive to revolution. The world of copies comprised industrially produced commodities distributed through advertising, arcades and department stores whose hegemonic infiltration of Parisian society would increasingly stifle desire for change. For Benjamin, Blanqui's assertion that endless repetition means zero progress is to be taken as an indictment of modernity's conjuring trick of concealing beneath a veneer of commodities what would be genuinely beneficial change. Those commodities stand as the illusory emblem of prosperity achieved through industrialisation and technological change, their newness and glamour disguising the wreckage just below the surface.

I don't know that I'm smart enough to draw a parallel with the hyper-commodification of contemporary art, much as I'd like to. I want instead to propose that Blanqui's infinity of replicas might be a key to countering the rampant speculation on artists and signature artworks that continues quite irrationally through one financial crisis after another. With the expansion of commodity distribution systems—aka galleries, museums and art fairs—you would be reasonable in thinking that the proliferation of artworks is in the realm of copies. At the same time that we are constantly manipulated by the business of art to think that it matters a lot who has made the artwork, that same marketplace occasionally provides the opportunity for indifference. The white noise of Frieze Art Fair, for example, where the status and authorship of thousands of works are levelled by the equality of display systems and by the duplication or similarity to one another of the works themselves, makes for extreme dehierarchisation. There is a sense in which you must leave your old criteria of value at the door and start from scratch to evaluate what is there, if you have the stamina. In spite of gallerists' efforts, the replication-virus of the fair structure undermines the likelihood of work being grasped in its singularity. Instead the rule of copies gets underway. A good thing in my view, for replication and multiplicity should destabilise confidence in value and speculation.

I wonder if Foucault's desubjectivising term 'author function' would be any use to us here. In questioning the status allocated to creative subjects, Foucault's 'author function' suggests working positions become available for writers, artists, their fans and their critics to create discourses in which, rather than becoming more visible as unique subjects, they increasingly disappear. As he puts it at the very end of the 1969 lecture "What Is an Author?", this shift in perspective enables useful questions to be asked: "What are the modes of existence of this discourse? Where has it been used, how can it circulate, and who can appropriate it for himself? [herself?]... Behind all these questions, we would hear hardly anything but the stirring of an indifference: What difference does it make who is speaking?" (p120, Foucault Reader, Pantheon).

As with Frieze Art Fair and with the 'author function' there is a similar evacuation of criteria of authorship needed in order to put up with the many films that fictionalise the lives of artists, or painters, as is usually the case. And in some of these films we readily find discourses laid open for examination or occupation as the roles played by these actor-artists, and the work they make on film, have significance neither for speculative financial, nor academic, investment. Paintings occur in these films as parodies of typical practice. These sequences are cartoons of art making. In the last century French caricaturists like Grandville and Cham parodied academic and avant-garde milieus. There is clearly something of the awareness of the behaviour of 19th-century commodities about these paintings in Grandville's illustrations that reach out to grab the spectator. But the closest I can find in this sphere to what I'm imagining here is the Dadaist parody cartoon of a dog shitting on the sleeping artist's canvas. These cartoons and films show that for any attempt at art making there are myriad impersonations that offer slight to extreme variations on the model. Since infinite variations of any artwork are imaginable, if not currently existent, it seems to me this offers different premises for exhibiting art. A show, for example, of work associated by its close similarities regardless of origin and motive (Art Rite cartoon and Krebber painting), or a show of work made for film, with or without any standard art examples alongside.

When actual historical artists are depicted in serious cinema the emphasis tends to be on conceptualisation, on thought. Pasolini, Tarkovsky, and Watkins show the painter driven by visions, by historical trauma, by family tragedy, but seldom working. Pasolini in *The Decamaron*, 1970, casts himself as a follower of Giotto as he wakes to a hallucination of the Virgin Mary presiding over the entrance to Hell. However, in other films about artists we are introduced to the figure of the clown where it's the dysfunctional use of tools that marks artists as humorous and unstable characters. The misuse of tools offers opportunity for physical comedy but also becomes the demonstrable point of a different worldliness, a counter-productivity. In *Ronald Neame's The Horse's Mouth,* 1958, (best known for Alec Guinness in the role of painter Gulley Jimson) and Tony Hancock's *The Rebel,* 1961, Paul Cox's *Man of Flowers,* 1983, Martin Scorsese's *Life Lessons,* 1989, Joel and Ethan Coens' *The Big Lebowski,* 1998, the actor-artists are conspicuously shown using brush, spray can, rope, feet, even a bicycle, to display a ludicrous physicality to art making. But what if these scenes were read not as dismissible farce but as the fractured double of actual studio practices, and as such doubles no less thorough an unveiling of masculinist tropes than what is achieved by the 'real' art mentioned at the start? This talk proposes that these cinematic representations be taken as implausible models for studio tool use, as a selection of an infinite number of instances that could be used to distort and unsettle the boundaries of acceptable practice.

The action paintings made by Hancock in *The Rebel,* by the painter in *Man of Flowers* and by Julianne Moore in *The Big Lebowski* are farcical, even embarrassing to watch and dismissible as ridiculous parodies of contemporary practice. They also show the artists' absurd use of tools, for this adds to the slapstick and allows artwork and artist to be immediately designated by the misuse of equipment, rather then some less transparent set of signifiers. I realise there are obvious precedents for the painting treatments in each film and that those original iterations exact an important erosion of dominant models, whether through the aristocratic effeteness and tool and method subversion of Yves Klein and Lucio Fontana, the immediacy of Gutai's material experiments, or, in relation to *The Big Lebowski,* the feminist performances of Shigeko Kubota and Lynda Benglis. In another longer talk these would have to be explained alongside the films as a widening theatre of critical carnivalesque painting. [Show the films...]

Although the way that these artworks are made, the way the tools are used, has a role in the film narratives and in establishing characters, as painting performance events their qualities exceed the needs of the films. Their autonomy as scenes increases with appropriations from contemporary painting practices, to which they attempt to naturalize by accretion some truly odd characteristics. It is these additional characteristics which make the events feel forced to those of us already involved in the flow of art making, but which I feel offer vectors of optimism or despair, depending on your orientation towards contemporary art practices.

It is a function of the art world's economic model to open up new markets and new types of commodities while holding that otherwise inexhaustible supply to principles of scarcity. At any moment it is a negligible amount of examples that are exhibited as art in comparison to the sphere of existing things. Blanqui quotes from Pascal's statement that "The entire visible world is nothing but an imperceptible stroke of the pen within the wide embrace of nature". And so it is with art, where the great variety of work on show in galleries, museums and fairs is only ever a tiny fraction of what is currently being made; it is an even smaller fraction of what doesn't think itself art but might become so; and it is a negligible fraction of what is still unimaginable future art that lies outside our current physiological or intellectual capabilities of discernment. What has risen to visibility has done so, we believe, by possessing relevancy, timeliness and qualities that other works lack. It is perhaps work that is more interesting to look at, think about, or listen to. Yet even in our world that small amount of visible art is mirrored by so much other work and has so many imitators and forerunners, that it is swept up by its author-function to be part of discourses, as Foucault explains, where the artworks, good and not so good, are ultimately interchangeable. And at that point it becomes more interesting to find the stranger works, the ones with inexplicable aberrations, those lacking author subjects, the ones which are missing out on relevancy and on timeliness, the ones that misbehave, or get misunderstood.

I'm suggesting that we take these film paintings as part of that aberrant world that challenges art-making proscriptions. Their author-functionality is complicated as they are a team production proposed in fiction as the work of one delusional subject. They act intoxicated routines of variously energetic work that typify a field of performance painting close enough to common practice to distortedly mirror the real thing. Their value as warped replicas should bring them closer to the world of actual exhibited art objects which they interpret. Amelia Jones notes the exclusion from commentary on Pollock's studio and painting of his male body and of any domestic context for the work, in spite of references to the methods used. "I continue to get further away from the usual painter's tools", Pollock says, "such as easel, palette, brushes etc. I prefer sticks, trowels, knives and dripping fluid paint". That these film works are all made in studios that double as domestic spaces where the banality of everyday life intrudes, where telephones get answered, drinks and food are consumed, bicycles and animals are kept, where pyjamas double as work clothes, to some extent renders the male studio permeable to the world of relationships, money and other everyday realities.

Jones points out how critics Harold Rosenberg and Clement Greenberg repressed the body that made the work, Pollock's male, heterosexual, masterful, agile, and violent body, while elaborating on its product, the gestures and actions that became the ostensible work's content. By contrast in the Hancock and Cox films the painter's body is clumsy and flabby, clowning around the canvas. If we can accept that the 'author-function' of the artist Pollock comprises the critical opinions of Rosenberg and Greenberg as well as the enthusiastic endorsements of Alan Kaprow and the kind of critical reprise made by Klein in his Anthropometries paintings, we should add the representations by Hancock, Cox and Coen Brothers, even if they are largely parodic. The clown's role is a anti-authorial one, anonymously played in lavish face-painted disguise, where the comedy parts are interchangeable within the troupe. There is neither writer nor text, just interchangeable roles and routines. That the paintings in the films of Hancock, Cox and the Coens could have been done by any clown further destabilises the prioritisation of the subject painter.

One of Joseph Kosuth's criticisms against painting in his essays from the late 70s/early 80s concerned its formal and procedural stasis and its narcissistic reflexivity. Painting was morphologically repetitive, too willing to concede political engagement and criticality to an easily interpreted visual delectation. Within that safe enclave painting was unable to locate an external position from where it might be alarmed at its vacuity and market complicity. At around the same time, Mary Kelly's essay "Re-viewing Modernist Criticism" instructed artists to better understand the market conditions whereby they complied with the directive for "signature gestures", as she put it, by which subjectivity enhanced art's commodity value. With better understanding of these processes, Kelly wrote, artists might succeed in developing alternative art practices.

I discern a sustained morphological similarity to Kosuth's conceptual practice that amounts to a signature style and through the authoritative positions and strong articulation of both artists it's possible to claim that a prominent subjectivity exerts its branding effect across their work. Differently perhaps, but no less effectively than with the painting they criticise. From the early 80s another celebrated criticism of painting's status quo suggested that instead of exiting the discipline, subterfuge within painting was the only viable strategy. In 'Last Exit: Painting' Tom Lawson's claim that "The appropriation of painting as a subversive method allows one to place critical aesthetic activity at the center of the marketplace, where it can cause the most trouble" seems hopelessly problematic, not least for allowing the writer and friends to continue showing their work in prominent galleries with critical immunity. The self-assertive actions of these artist critics in using positions of authority to cordon off from relevance large areas of practice is business as usual for experts and as such has negligible impact on deflecting the manner and velocity of art commerce.

The possibility of finding artwork that is unrecuperable by market or criticality (the same thing in many cases) seems slim until one looks at practices that are beneath visibility, that have no interest in being recognised by the art profession, and which are inherently worthless according to the terms of that profession. Would exhibiting such works, even granting them the scrutiny they get in a talk like this, just draw them into the same vortex of commerce that envelops the "outsider" art of Massimiliano Gioni's Biennale and other cabinet of curiosity shows of this last year? Or perhaps that is not where they are best put to use, that their current status as outside, unworthy, false representations is what is of value. Perhaps the criteria that determine their value, or lack of it, need better articulation. An aesthetics of distaste and ruin perhaps. Do they appall us because they recuperate, make fun of rebellion, and present our own serious efforts as quite possibly embarrassingly shambolic, our own cutting edge social practices, institutional critique, even critique itself as possibly, as quite likely, ridiculous?

In case the negative function of this anti-art movie paintings seems completely implausible I want to mention an earlier fantasy that makes this nightmare of cinema art more interesting. Amongst the labyrinthine narratives of Superman comics is author Otto Binder's concept of Bizarro Superman. Initiated by evil mastermind Lex Luthor to generate an equally powerful opponent to Superman, the Bizarro genetics project goes wrong and what emerges is a confused double of Superman whose goals, values and language he mirrors in inverse form. Justifying why he is selected to solve a crime the mayor compliments Bizarro by explaining it is "Because you are stupider than the entire Bizarro police force put together". In their broken language Bizarro citizens acclaim "Us do opposite of all Earthly things! Us hate beauty! Us love ugliness! Is big crime to make anything perfect on Bizarro World!"

These fake art films, I suggest, can be viewed as a Bizarro world of art, a flawed mirror image, in which follies are played out imperfectly, like warped variants of real art life. Bizarro returns us to Blanqui's duplicate planets As he explains: "Progress here is only for our nephews...Children of a better humanity, they have already scoffed at us and mocked us on dead earths, passing there before us. From living earths from which we have disappeared they continue to condemn us; and on earths to be born, they will forever pursue us with their contempt".

The aesthetic radicalisms that burst out at regular intervals to attempt to disrupt the process of commercial exchange always fall back into the dismal history of this relationship of power, money and art. These radicalisms are in many ways simply parts of a mosaic comprising a complex socio-economic image that requires inventiveness and authenticity (as if these were brands) to vindicate its projection of purpose. Rebellion is part of the code that constitutes this economic-aesthetic relationship. Blanqui's terrifying vision encompasses all of these nuances of revolt as already foretold facets of infinite variation and repetition. Nevertheless, we cherish moments of difference amongst these artworks and ideas. Slacker artists play this dismal relationship to the brink. Remember Mike Kelley's remark that had he known how nasty the art world was he'd have chosen another profession. The notion is well taken that all artistic acts take place in front of and part of this phantasmagoria, whether as celebrations of its form, as rebellious opposition where they mirror the form in negative, or as indifferent stupid undergrounds drifting away into irrecuperability.

READINGS FROM 'ARTICULATING THE EVENT SPACE' BY PETER LEWIS
PETER FILLINGHAM

PF   I'm Peter Fillingham. I'm a friend of Peter Lewis and I'm very proud to sit in for him today. He asked me to come along today to read out some extracts from his text.

I am a sculptor and collaborator and curator and having worked in education a lot. And my knowledge of this environment and the context of John Latham came very much from conversations with John, in Paris over breakfasts. And I'm interested in all the links between people and things. In teaching sculpture, strangely, and trying to bring new people to sculpture as a host, I started showing these extracts from the television programme *Out of Town* with Jack Hargreaves. And when you make 'traditional country things' you tend to use tools in a very interesting way and one of my main objectives there, was to show people how to create tools out of the things around them. And to make things. And to invent tools, which I think is very important. But the main objective is to slow down the velocity of thinking and to slow down the whole way of looking. And I think that's a really important part of thinking about tools – so it's about time itself and how to slow time down.

I'm going to read out a few of Peter's extracts from his text – but I think the voice itself is also a tool of course and mine is actually fading – but thinking about Francis Alÿs' work – and working and looking at the mould as a thing that breaks down, everytime you create from a mould you create a copy – but the pragmatics of teaching while making and using a mould is that it breaks down, just as we break down – the voice also breaks down, which for me is an ongoing situation – –

1. *The origins are arguably aligned in the relationship of Alexander Dorner's 'museum on the move' with the nomadic avant-gardist Kurt Schwitters, whose works were produced on the run. In 'The Institution is dead! Long live the institution!', Claire Doherty quotes from Samuel Cauman's Living*

Museum: Experiences of an Art Historian: 'Dorner first posited the notion of a "museum on the move" and famously suggested, "the new type of art institute cannot merely be an art museum as it has been until now, but no museum at all. The new type will be more like a power station, a producer of new energy."'

2. Both tilted the conception of how art might not only survive 'outside', but how it is to be brought into singular existence. Defined by Gregory Sholette as a kind of dark matter, an avant-garde has now no specific site of situation or possibility of negation – since capitalism is somehow the cause of everything, but it is also this elusive phlogiston that is every-where and nowhere. In a 'worldless' context, radical art runs the risk, as Hal Foster has said, of a 'weird formalism', of discursivity and sociality pursued for its own sake. And as Boris Groys notes, that to perform at the level of the universal where a demand to be artists tends more toward a dystopian reality imposed by the perversity of the Superego injunction to 'enjoy.' We are all artists by demand. Marc James Léger writes: 'What we get with all the talk of horizontalism and participatory democracy proposes only the democratic form of struggle against capitalism. This belief in democratic form tends to repudiate universality and class politics and becomes an ultrapolitics that depoliticizes the conflicts that are generated by the radical right.'

3. Negation is always, in its concrete action – political or artistic – suspended between destruction and subtraction. That the very essence of negation is destruction has been the fundamental idea of the last century. The fundamental idea of the beginning century must be that the very essence of negation is subtraction.' Alain Badiou (2007) Destruction, Negation, Subtraction – on Pier Paolo Pasolini.

4. What happens when we can't see the edges of these legitimising networks, positions and policies? Belief grows stronger when held at a distance, or close up, as the 'hidden' fetish blurred in the guise of scepticism; one may allocate a third place for 'new' resistances in the middle, between destruction and subtraction, to produce the active part of negation of any situation.

5. Of the descendants of Institutional Critique Fraser writes: 'It is not possible to evaluate the work of ... any of the artists whose work proceeds from theirs without taking into account not only the visible, visual manifestations of their practices, but also their policies; not only of the artistic positions they manifest, but also of the positions they construct for themselves within the network of relations that constitutes the fields of their activities.'

6. Curating is as divisive as it is shared, 'supposed-to-know', if representing artists. Different urban contexts and agents share yet divide up the score. Curators and commentators alike find comfort in speculative notions like that of Bourdieu's collective 'global intellectual', whereby local actors undertake their work as part of a global initiative, the danger being the benign restoration of a conservatism that provides an alibi to capitalism.

7. Bruno Latour and Weibel (as curators) will use an academically sanctioned curatorial authority, as an alibi legitimated by historiography, to present an assemblage/package, from the territorialised space of the museum. They aim to reassemble pragmatism from their research. Conducted over many years the work initiates a productive use of the museum, reconfigured as a 'life-space.' The constellation of practices that invoke 'life', re-presenting archives or documents as part of the theatricality of a museum spectacle, employing rigorous deterritorialisations, might make the move from avant-garde as a resource to being about its limitations.

8. Without relying on such rhetorical commentaries aimed to attack the objects of curating – the art versus the 'what is supposed to know, but pretends (not to know) itself (curating)', i.e. the curator disguises the discourse it works with, supports an event outside 'curating', as a purer discourse precisely since it is unformatted – to being really about the logic of sustaining the fiction of curatorial professionalism, by expanding the fiction of definition, re-drawing lines between art works and their organisation and what is not to be regarded worthwhile. Exploiting the event's 'inexistence' is therefore to maintain its questionability. There is one proper formalisation of an emergence, to speak from the object, and not to it, to create realpolitik from the myth of an existence (of an avant-garde) literally out of its inexistence. The object will have appeared when it does, or doesn't, at any given time, anywhere, but the occasion is to be highly localised, being part of a whole formation, and yet not included as part. Unity, incompleteness and 'the universal' fight in discursive

attention to, and distract attention from, the object. The event emerges thus eternally bruised in the ruins of its embattled networks. Being 'premature', it is unformatted, since always intentionally not fully formed or complete. The series – the essence of event-based practice – is a form of infinite taxonomy. On one side it is an infinite reference document of reproduced materials, on the other the shifting horizon of signified qualities based as individual examples, and elevated through protracted multiplications.

9. Amid the detritus of idealisms, the invasive new tools of post 'post-critical' media are put to use. The ethic in any re-composition of the body and politics remains unanswered or falls, as must be done, having no choice. One deceives oneself by abstractions that permit or sanction the access to the real, which remains out of reach.

10. 'To raise a political question often means to reveal a state of affairs whose presence was hitherto hidden. But then you risk falling into the same trap of providing social explanations and do exactly the opposite of what is meant here by political flow. You use the same old repertoire of already-gathered social ties to "explain" the new associations. Although you seem to speak about politics you don't speak politically. What you are doing is simply the extension one step further of the same small repertoire of already standardised forces. You might feel the pleasure of providing a "powerful explanation", but that's just the problem: You yourself partake in the expansion of power not the re-composition of its content.'

11. What it does is not block composition. It might try to contain or contaminate the multiple practices that issue forth more multiples into a 'worldless' excess or subjectless condition. Like precious objects hidden in a worthless box, the practice cannot present outside its expanding content, if there is no subject, world. We have to learn something of nihilistic subjectivity. Every object is – the outside and its infinite incomplete or inconsistent 'whole' – a kind of astonishment within a wooden banality. A certain grace is lost to culturalisation. So the curator is at the mercy of repeating himself voluntarily, subtracting something new from the repetitions he contemplates.

These extracts are a selection from a range which make some of the connections that Peter and I have been talking about. And there is a small part from my Jimmie Durham book which I thought would be quite nice to end on. It's the *Interview with a 10,000 Year Old Artist*. And the question is – this is a two-part question –

Q: How would you describe your work? And what do you think of modern art?

A: I guess I'd say I'm a traditionalist. I work in the classical style that has proven value over the centuries. I like some of the modern painters, Tischen for example. But they need more discipline, and a sense of quality, with lasting value. Political work, that is paintings that are pushing some ideology of the moment, such as Christianity, cannot possibly hold up after the fad is over. As a traditionalist I also question the use of all of this new material and media. I'm very suspicious of oil paint, especially when it is applied to this flimsy cloth they all love to use, stretched over flimsy sticks. I don't think oil on canvas has been around long enough to be proven yet. What's wrong with painting on a good solid cave wall. Or a tough buffalo hide? All the experiments with new media show a poverty of ideas. But this guy, Keith Haring, his work might last.

Q: What would you say is the biggest problem as an artist?

A: Family life, definitely. I've had 100 kids and my husband thinks I should stay in a cave.

Anyway that's my contribution.

VERBATIM TRANSCRIPTION

LEARNING TO USE ONE ANOTHER
ALEX SCHADY

AS   My name is Alex Schady. I'm not going to say very much, instead I'm going to show you some things and just respond to them. The reason that I'm here matters as it came out of a series of discussions that Peter Lewis and I had. I work at Central Saint Martins and Peter is the external there, and we'd been talking about how art schools have changed in this country over the years. What the problems or possibilities for it were. And when Peter asked me to do this I didn't have a set of thought out responses to the theme of tools. I did, however, have a question that was repeatedly asked of me when I made work and that was the accusation that I used people as tools. And that was always seen as a problem. It was always something that was to be questioned in the work. And not something that was positive. And I just wondered whether I could start to think of that as actually a positive stance and one that might be developed, not just within my own practice but within an art institutions. Whether using each other as tools could be something that challenged power relationships between staff and students.

So I'm just going to show you a few films and talk a little bit about them.

[video projection of *He made me do it*] - a group of children wearing masks are sat in a classroom. Different sets of children stand up point at the camera and say 'he made me it' do before once again sitting down. The piece repeats with different groupings of children standing up and making their accusation.

I was working with Tate Learning on a year-long project with a group of teachers that explored how gallery education might inform primary school teaching models. It was a long project and at the end of it I asked if it was ok for me to go back into the schools and produce a piece of work. Tate were happy for me to do that, it was all agreed, and then I produced this piece of work that became very problematic. To their credit they supported me but they were very anxious about it. The parents that came to see the piece were cross, or some of them were. And the thing they said to me was, you're just using our children as tools. And that in itself was seen as a problem.

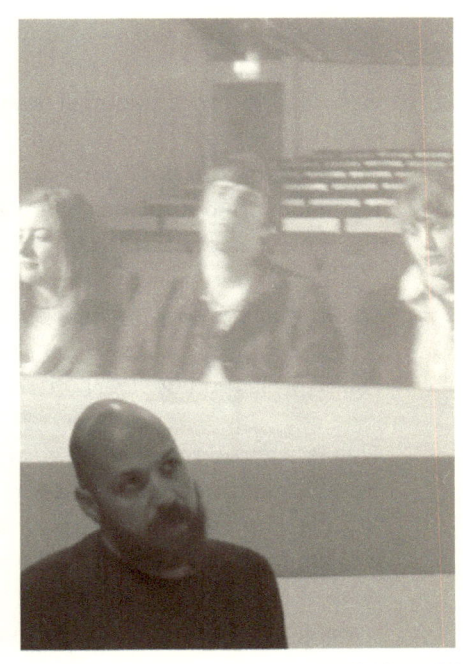

ALEX SCHADY

I felt what the piece was trying to do was to declare the relationship that exists between the artist and the participants in this sort of socially engaged/ gallery education project, where an artist gets thrown into an alien environment and a piece of work is produced. It concerned me that there seemed to be an expectation for these projects to provide creative freedom for the participants (what ever that might mean) – that what the artist was there to do was to offer up a sense of freedom. I wanted to make apparent the lack of choice offered to the pupils in this work. I don't think offering greater choice necessarily improves the experience for collaborators in these sorts of projects.

I want to briefly mention another project where Id been invited to make a piece of work with the staff in a call centre. When I arrived the manager of the centre sat myself and the other filmmaker down and he said "well we've had a meeting before you arrived; we've all had a big chat and what we've decided we'd like you to make is a sculpture that will be 3 gorillas with their hands outstretched and then we can all sit on the gorilla hands" And it might have been a great piece – it sounds cool, but it wasn't the piece that I was going to make. And that was how they saw what our function was. And I think with *He made me do it* the parents very much saw that as well. They wanted me to provide a model where the pupils offered up the content of the work and that didn't interest me. I wanted to make something with the schools that would throw up interesting questions for everyone involved but I didn't see creative freedom as an important function in this The masks they are wearing, by the way, are meant to be pictures of me. Although they were slightly more colourful than I am!

I'll show you the next film – and I apologise for showing examples of my own work but it was the only way I could get into discussing this. The next piece wasn't problematic at all. And I want to discuss the distinction between one and the other and why this one was felt to be so difficult and why the next one had no problems associated to it.

[video projection *Boulder*]

This is a group of secondary school students here. And its a piece of work I made in collaboration with someone else. And I think that's slightly what made it more palatable. They're rolling a boulder through a town, from the main museum of the town, down a high street to the edge of the town. And they've got placards up. And all the placards are making statements that are against stasis or against petrification. They are following our instructions – the way in which the placards are made is following our instructions, the way in which the text is applied is to our instructions. However they have the freedom to decide on the language that was used on the placards themselves. So the nature of the statement, although what they were saying – 'No To Stasis', 'No To Petrification' – the nature of statements is their own. And that in a sense completely defused it because anybody coming to this place, anybody discussing this would talk to the individual student and ask them why they chose that particular statement. And as limited as that freedom was it was enough to take the focus away from myself and Hadas Kedar (the other artist), in terms of our absurd megalomania in that we created this fictitious ritual where the boulder is rolled through the town – it's a small town in Norway in the north, Sandnes.

So I wanted to bring this sort of work into the university context, I wanted to see what happened when you bring it in there. And of course the added problem of the power relationship within the university is that when you're doing something for gallery education you're not assessing anything – you're not giving them a grade at the end of that process, you're just telling the 'oh we're all marvellous isn't that good.' And so I decided it would be interesting to see what happened if I abused the students in a more active way. So I produced a piece of work in which the students –

[video projection *Intermission*]

Here I'm in a lecture theatre in front of a group of students who have volunteered to be part of this. So there's only about 10 students or maybe 15; and they sit at the front of the lecture theatre. And all I've told them is that they're coming to take part in a piece of work that's my own piece of work. They will be performers in this. And that whatever happens in this space, they're not to take it personally. And I sit them down and I film them and I tell them they're dreadful. And I tell that they're middle class bourgeois students who have never had any urgency about what they're making and all their work has been a waste of time, although they think they know what they're doing it's all just purile nonsense. And I have a real go at them for about half an hour. They're remarkable stoic through it, although they start giggling and whispering half way through. And that then became the basis for a performance that we did in the oil tanks, when the oil tanks opened. And for that one students took control over me. So although I came up with the text and I'm abusing them in this film, the students, through a process of clicking on a computer, get to choose what bit of the text is being read out by me. So they can control what abuse I'm hurling at this new audience. And there was something that Suzanne Lacy said about who the author was at various moments that really started to interest me in terms of this idea of the students as the tool. That if I'm presenting the work, I'm happy to present this as my work. If the students – and everyone is given access to the work, and I'm very suspicious of any sort of claim that the work is in any sense democratic but I do offer them the piece as video footage and they can do whatever they want with it, I'm not concerned with that. If they show the work they can claim it as their own. And if I show the work I absolutely claim it as my own and I don't call them my collaborators, I call them my tools. And I think that's important. There's a sense in which, just by claiming a collaborative process that you can – you can have a relationship that of course is filled with problematic power relations but you just don't declare it because you say 'we're all involved in this together isn't it marvellous.' But as the artist you're the one who's making them do it – like the first film where the students declare it 'he made me do it' and even that is constructed by me, I'm making them say it. And I'm making them say it in particular orders.

I'm going to come on to a last couple of image – and this is not my work – its something that Winchester School of Art and and Central Saint Martins collaborated on. It's Louisa Minkin and Ian Dawson, Winchester School of Art and Mick Finch at Saint Martins. Louisa had become very interested in Francois Willeme's Photo Sculpture Machine which is – in 360 degrees there are these series of panels, within each panel there's a camera, the camera takes a picture of the person in the middle and those pictures are then used by a mechanism like that [picture] so you end up with this way of producing a sculpture. The sculptures themselves are completely – they're beautiful but they don't really mimic the subject, they're very crude, they get certain things right and then it falls apart. But it was definitely – it started off as a project when Louisa wanted to build this thing and she had no space or recourse to build it and so she brought it to me and what we decided to do was get the students to build it for her. The students provided the manpower, the students provided the skills, provided their space in their studio to build it and there was no pretence that this wasn't going to be for Louisa. Some of the footage shows they are using cranes and tracking that they used to help film the process and that's something that I got them to do but again it was not initially constructed for their benefit however they then have access to these things. They then can use these things in any way they want. We're not interested. We got what we wanted out of it. We've used the students. Got what we wanted. And of course that's declared to the students – we say to the students 'we are developing this project, Louisa's project is this, it will be her work, who wants to jump on board?' And the students that want to are the ones that take advantage of it. Any student can then use the equipment – and this is a question and I don't think I've come up with a sensible answer for it, the question was, is there a way in which instrumentalising each other, staff to students and students to staff – and I guess what I haven't shown is how students can instrumentalise staff and that might be something we want to discuss further on, maybe that's the next step – but how there might be potential there to destabilise some of those inherent hierarchies that exist within those institutions. And the power relationships that exist within those institutions. I guess on a certain level its bound to failure and assessment is the reason you have this failure because at the end of the day there's someone judging some one else for a particular grade. But I think there are things we can do along the way to challenge that and question that and throw that on its head. But I think it could be very interesting and that's all I have to say. Thank you.

VERBATIM TRANSCRIPTION
OPEN FLOOR DISCUSSION

AB   We are hoping that we can pick up on some of the things that people have said and anyone (audience) can bring something to the conversation, that'd be ideal. I don't have an introduction per se but I'm going to try'n make some links between what everybody was saying. And it seemed there were a couple of things that over-lapped. So the idea of systems or relations – systems of value and power, systems of production, especially in the first couple of talks – and then moving on, ideas of copies and repetition, also the author function in relation to tools. One thing that I thought was very interesting in your talk Verina, was the idea of post-production and it made me think of this quote that I had been thinking about, it's from the latest e-flux article by Hito Steyerl, *Too Much World: Is the Internet Dead?*, so she's talking about post-internet, she says, "Under these conditions, production morphs into post-production, meaning the world can be understood but also altered by its tools. The tools of post-production: editing, colour correction, filtering, cutting, and so on are not aimed at achieving representation. They have become means of creation, not only of images but also of the world in their wake." So I was just very interested in this – the process of the interview that you (Verina) spoke about and in particular this idea of post-production – the negotiation, editing, reformatting involved in that process and also how the interview goes through these various value systems, almost similar to the *Seven Lives of Garbage* work by Alÿs. So, primarily being a proposal in the first instance that becomes an exchange that leads to a transcript that leads to a publication which is a book, which is a product. So I don't know if you want to talk more about that or if you've said everything you had to say?

VG   I agree the interview itself, the actual conversation is malleable – in terms of material agency, if you like. And whatever is involved in editing, which I think over the last few years became an expanded practice so to speak, this 'editing' involves all kinds of things, reading, interpreting, selecting, extracting, but also leaving out. And for me most interesting is to also think about, 'Where is the place of the thing?' I mentioned that before that whatever it is it shapes, it co-produces the very context – –

AS   I was taking as you were speaking then, that it's not just the post-production that's an expanded field, it's in the world of Skype and telephone interviews and however else we might do it, that the interview itself has become an expanded practice. And I was thinking about Errol Morris' approach to interviewing where rather than sitting in front of the person he's interviewing, he'll have a monitor in front of himself and a monitor in front of the interviewee with a live feed, so you're only ever talking to the television version of the person you're interviewing, as a way of producing some distance. And I think there's something about the way in which that interview, or the possibility for the interview itself has shifted dramatically in the last 10 years.

VG   But also its status in the market place – who spoke about market and distribution etc? I mean the interview is probably not the same any more, as it was 20 years ago. Its place in the art world, in contemporary art, in terms of knowledge and informal knowledge and what we understand about knowledge production. And again – the most notorious interviewers, Hans Ulrich Obrist – you can think about interviewing in very different terms, I mean what he's doing is mainly to look, to speak to artists he's interested in – it's always a different angle to interviewing, as such, which also involves different processes and different post-production.

AS   And then we also have the film about the interview, the Nixon/Frost interview. And that in itself has become – –

MH   That's - it seems to me the flaws within that medium - it seemed that the objective - or how that particular exchange was valued was that Frost was able to elicit a confession from Nixon, so there's a sense in which the interview on that level is intended to reveal something that's concealed. And typically that's not such a primary objective with artists' interviews which, I think you indicated, has more to do with the construction or the furthering of careers. The construction of artists' identities. And not something that was intended to trip the artist up into making a mistake or revealing something that's not – –

VG   But also this idea of fictionalising the artist's practice like what Antonia talked about - in terms of Frieze (art fair) – or Mark was talking about.

AMR   Also I think you (Verina) mentioned something about the interviews being a matter of time. I was wondering, can you speak a little bit more about how you see this interview as being an issue of time, which I find really fascinating.

VG   In what sense?

AMR   I don't know, that's why I wanted to ask.

AB   You (Verina) said it's an event, which I suppose is the same thing.

VG   Yeah interesting, the interview obviously has a lot to do with what has not yet been discussed or has not yet been revealed in someone's work or life. So it's kind of both in the past and in the future. So it's looking backwards but also projecting into the future. That's one issue I'm quite interested in, especially for example with the Negri interview, I went back to that time in '68 with these publications and his involvement with these journals and it's a side of Negri which is not yet in the public sphere. And for him – he then told me that he agreed to the interview precisely because of that. He was just researching this time, for him, in his life he had to just cover up, for political reasons, but also for personal emotional reasons.

AMR   I think that is really interesting because I feel – some other examples as you were speaking, especially in contemporaneity, Christine Ross's book *The Past is the Present, It's the Future Too,* which is all about contemporary art practices which try to bring the past closer to the present and future. To conflate and produce new temporal models perhaps as a way to resist heavily formatted or very straightforward notions of time, so I just thought it was really interesting that – because I hadn't really seen the interview as a matter of time, especially, as you were saying, there's been a whole outburst of interviews. And interviews have become the format for a lot of contemporary artists and it treads a very fine line between self-advertisement and actual interviewee – finding new knowledge and so forth.

VG   But maybe there is also this aspect of a certain intimacy inherent to the interview, and at the same time it's already public, what you are doing. I'm quite interested in that level as well. Because obviously you share this time with a particular person and you touch upon certain things which are not constructed beforehand and not anticipated beforehand.

MH   There's an aspect of what you're say where Negri agrees to be interviewed by someone who is knowledgeable about his background, someone who has already invested time and scholarship in it, and there was some years ago the concept of the star interviews, the star artist being interviewed by the star interviewer. And the artist declining interviews that don't produce an event. And the case I'm thinking of is Luc Tuymans being interviewed by T. J. Clark in America and hundreds and hundreds of people attended in a great hall and you would expect something penetrating from an interview like that, but actually I find with Clark, the closer he gets to the present day the less effective he is or the less interesting he is as a commentator; and so it was in this instance where none of the questions were sufficiently probing to elicit anything except a new form of adulation of Tuymans. As an event it was successful, especially as it coincided with a one person show of Tuymans.

AS   I think it's also intriguing - thinking about celebrity status - as the interview in popular culture recedes - and I might just be making this up but it seems to me that your Oprah's, you know, those big interview formats that were on TV, that moment of the mass celebrity interview seems to be falling back and it's as that's happening, as it's loosing some purchase on popular culture that it becomes something very important in the art world, and whether there's any relationship there?

PF   I was brought up in a generation of watching television - face-to-face interviews on television; look at Alan Whicker and the questions he asks - back to Mark's point, it's all about the intelligent person who's done his homework and the interview is actually a very intelligent place, and I think this sense that the history is not taught and the history is not acknowledged, these momentary celebrity things do not represent for me anything apart from taking a particular moment to be sold. Thinking about a Frieze (art fair) way of looking at it – it's so particular of a moment and of course that takes away all of the intelligence that I enjoy when I look at certain interviews. I've looked at many interviews which were not about speed, like Graham Norton's show is now - and the... [transcript interruption] ...interview by Chuck Close, it just shows another way which is not so fast, which is not about celebrity. I think it challenges the lack of history that's allowed to come in. A Hans Ulrich Obrist type of interview is of a particular moment.

CL   Do you think there's a difference between interviewing, let's say an artist and interviewing somebody who is an historical/political figure, like Negri? If you're relying on his memory, as you spoke about, and also I think you spoke about the deformation of history, where – it's possible you have an obligation to some kind of idea of historical objectivity to things that happened at that time and also to negotiate his unintentional or intentional, or his personal desires to portray that particular history in a certain way. I mean he would have to be an amazingly objective person to not bring his own desires to that retelling. I mean if you're interviewing an artist then well, you know, it's fine if they reconfigure what happened – during the break we were talking about Philip Auslander who talks about the reactivation of something through documentation, so considering this in relation to the historical figure that Negri is, it's (perhaps?) not ok, to reactivate and perhaps reinterpret that history, especially because of his pivotal role, or maybe it's more that it's just not possible to approach this type of interview in the same way as one would an interview with an artist – what do you think of that?

VG   I don't really understand your question.

CL   Whether there's a difference between, let's say, historical figures who – where an interview might have a certain currency in the domain of art but when you interview somebody in a different domain, in the domain of politics where peoples' lives have been effected, I guess, is there a different kind of currency?

VG   It's always very different I think, whatever profession the person you're interviewing has. It's less the profession of someone but, again, what is the main objective of interviewing this particular person.

AM   Is there an element of performance involved during an interview? Especially when interviewing someone like an artist who is very intimately involved with his work, he is almost a representative for it, so whatever he gives off through his body language or through what he says, it's as if – when we were talking about the tools for accessing knowledge, I guess we could consider the interview as a tool for accessing this knowledge, in a very literal sense. Where as you could interview someone who is maybe a scientist who has discovered something and we're not really interested in him as a person, we're interested in his discovery, so you would ask him historical questions of context so that we have a text book type of reference. I guess I'm interested in the interview as a tool to access things, because this happens spontaneously during the interview which you would've had expected.

VG   But also with an interview the person and the work and talk is always very close together. In a different encounter you might not have that. So on that level you can always see it as a performative act. And it can go pretty wrong as well.

AMR   Doesn't it run the risk of re-sneaking the author through the back door? Basically, of highlighting the figure of the artist, doer as a celebrity, culty person. And sometimes skewing the actual reading of the works. And it feels like, at least in art history, as a field we battled against that kind of interpretation of the artwork as relying on the artist's intentions, desires and so forth, for many years, but that now it seems to be biting us in the ass and sort of returning through the interview format as the artist as really the soul advertiser or soul validator. Very smartly, and very marketably, so not smartly, but with a view on self-promotion.

CL   It's kind of self-mythologising and it provides that platform to do that. And revisiting – which is fine, maybe it's fine, you know, as an artist.

AMR   Sure. It's just that my fear is that it will re-establish the cult of the artist, the figure of the artist as soul provider of meaning.

MH   There's the opportunity to misuse the tool. There's quite a nice example online, Kenny Everett interviewing Kate Bush, it's a very short sequence in which she is answering out of step with him so it makes no sense and at the end he says, "I've been speaking with Kate Bush and she's been speaking with someone else." But I think David Burrows did a wonderful interview with someone showing at the ICA, I can't remember who, and again they un-synced the two texts. And way back the critic Peter Fuller, famously in Art Monthly, interviewed, I think it was Carl Andre, and this was before email so the text was sent back and forth, and Peter Fuller came under massive criticism for altering what Andre said in the interview. He wasn't just correcting it, he was actually altering. So his respondent said, "This is not the question he asked me, I'm being misrepresented here," and I can see that as being a productive device.

VG   That's really a question of editorial decisions because Alex, who is quite a tough editor – I thought it's not the same interview any more, almost. He left out quite a lot of stuff which I think creates more 'life' in the interview. But that's totally specific to the actual interview – but these questions come up.

AS   I've been interviewed a few times for something that'll end up in print and I'm always amazed, because I know what I sound like and I know how banal my answers might've been like in the interview, when they come back to you, when they've been polished up by someone - they've caught the essence of what you're saying [laughter] but in that process it absolutely becomes something else.

AM   Did you make the interview in writing in the end, because you sent the question one week – –

VG   He said he wanted the questions in advance but when I arrived he said he didn't have time to look at them.

AM   And did you have to send the finished interview to him?

VG   Yes of course, he has to sign off.

MH   I was interested to have learned that in Italy – from a man who was deeply involved in the punk scene internationally – that in that period, in the 1970s – who I asked, "Where were the Italian punk bands?" because they exist in every other country. He was saying that it was extremely hard for musicians to do anything disruptive, not involved in radical left politics. And I think at one stage Lou Reed was prevented from playing in Florence. There was a very small number of punk bands and they were very brave because they would get their gigs smashed up and broken. When one thinks of these left movements as being in some manner liberatory but the opposite seems to be have been the case, where in Italy with certain forms of culture at that time – –

VG   It's quite a militant activism, so to speak, as well. Especially also in the actual conversation he (Negri) – there was this movement which is mentioned in his book *Multitude,* with Hardt, called 'The White Overalls.' This was a social centre activity in the 1970s, near Florence. And we discussed a little bit the social spaces at the time. And how they remained active, in resistance. And he said the police were just not let in those places, there was a barricade.

AM   I was just thinking about this work that you (Alex) did with your students. I felt that it was really like interviewing them in a way. I wonder could you have bad answers? Could they have reacted in a way that you would not have made the film in the end?

AS   That's interesting. I don't think so. I was fairly confident, given the remit of what I as doing, that there wasn't that much space for them to do something that would've been disruptive. And that's not because they couldn't have stood up and broken the camera – but given the relationship that you have with your students, given established power relationships you have with them, there are certain ways in which we all understand we're going to behave in a lecture. So I wonder – –

AM   They could be laughing the whole time.

AS   They laughed at one point, and I kept it in. The most disturbing version I've had in a lecture was when I gave some lectures in China where I was being translated, and I would say a sentence and the sentence would get translated, and they warned me before I went in that this particular group of students were working very hard and they use the lectures as a space to sleep and I had about 50% of the pupils completely asleep within 3 minutes of me starting. And that felt really extraordinary because it genuinely felt like it was doing something that was very challenging to what one imagined were the rules of this encounter.

AB   They disturbed the power relation. By sleeping they're refusing to enter into your process of exchange.

AS   Although on the one hand I'm interested in that power relation being confronted in that way, you know on the other hand I can't be that comfortable because the next day I warned them about this, "The last time a number of you fell asleep, I've got a camera in my pocket and I'm making a piece of work, anyone that falls asleep I'm going to take their photograph," and that kept a lot more of them awake.

AB   So you grabbed the power back.

AS   I know. I did. I guess for me it's always about declaring when I'm grabbing it back. And that doesn't make it ok but at least it acknowledges it. Because I think it's inevitable that you're within that power dynamic – –

CL   Do you feel that you're doubly in power because you're using the camera as well which is already this powerful tool and you're in this position of authority.

AS   Yeah, that was really manipulative of me, absolutely. And I had no confidence that these photographs would ever become anything other than something amusing to show colleagues when I got back. Which again is slightly suspect! [laughter]

AMR   I think it's really interesting – some of my research is on Santiago Sierra and his delegation and buying of performers time and body. So there are many resonances with the kind of work that you're trying to do, but yours seems to be somewhat less coercive in monetary terms but a little bit more coercive in ideological terms perhaps because your game is – they're not being paid for this in any way, shape or form. Their subjectivity is being very limited by the conditions that you give and in some projects they seem to go through this principal of individuation, this power the students either take on or not, I was wondering, in particular if the production of behaviour – because what you're playing with is the behaviour of other people, how far are you willing to go?

AS   I don't know, I was talking to someone during the break and I said the next piece I proposed to Tate after *He Made Me Do It,* was I wanted to go into a class room and gaffa tape the students to their chairs. And they said no but I'm still talking to them about possibly doing that. And I don't have an objective in mind, I don't think I want to get it to this stage. I don't think of myself as particularly – –

CL   Dangerous?

AS   No, not at all. It's like, here's a button, press it. It's almost, "I wonder what happens if I do this?," and I am deeply troubled by the power that I understand that I have within an educational context. I feel very uncomfortable with it – and we all know that we've moved away from the idea of a teacher having knowledge that they impart; but some of that still exists and it seems to me that what it's been replaced with now is equally problematic – one in which students understand entitlement and what they're entitled to. And these two things seem to conflate within these institutions and they are both deeply troubling in terms of the power dynamics that exist, and so I think it's because of an anxiety that I feel about them that I just keep needing to prod at it and see what happens.

VG   Is there also the question of responsibility, taking responsibility? So you're talking about power, or not having power, or giving up power, how this has changed but still it's lacking throughout. Nobody really wants to take responsibility, for whatever – –

AS   Yeah, because responsibility is dangerous. You're right and I think, again, that is very problematic. But we have to at least acknowledge that it's there. That for me seems to be the crux of it.

CL   Do you think that – it seems like you're walking this really delicate line and you're very aware of all of the issues involved in doing that but – I was looking at this video by Renzo Martens called *Enjoy Poverty* and so he's also walking this very – this line of the ethical dimension to what he's doing – so do you think there's a relationship between what he is doing and what you're doing?

AS   On a certain level - and I was told by someone who knows a lot better than me, that I should not mention the word 'ethics,' but on a certain level the question about the ethics of what you're doing in both cases is important. I think I'm probably within more comfortable territory because it's much less edgier, because it's so much the institution I'm within, that I don't have to take a position outside of it, so on that level it's easy. But I can understand there is an ethical dimension to both, yeah.

PF   As you were saying during the break, when you were talking about the fact that they were drawing you, that made a lot of resonance with Renzo Martens' film. It is very much, and he does declare this at the end, that it's a question of pride and vanity. He plays the whole 'wrath of God' type of anthropologist, the Fitzcarraldo thing all the way through, and that tiny thing that you (Alex) were saying that 'they were drawing me' – that does have a massive resonance I think in putting you absolutely on the spot, I'd say it's equally as dangerously, and probably even more dangerously if you're working somewhere like Tate. And I think the relationship between those two artists is actually really very interesting. I saw his film at a documentary film festival in a field and it brought the house down. There was a lot of violence going on between the journalism and the non-journalism. I think that it's a good artist to relate to Alex's work.

MH   I don't want to shift the discussion but I have a question for Andrés. I often wonder with Alÿs's work, who does the filming? And what's the relationship between the filmmaker and the artist? If you take someone like Bas Jan Ader we know who made the films. And he (Rene Daalder) made that wonderful recent film about his life *Here is Always Somewhere Else*. So if there wasn't a filmmaker there'd be no document, the work would be there but perhaps not written about.

AMR   This is perhaps one of the many problems with Alÿs's practice. It's very often doubted that he is the only maker. As if he was both walker and documenter at the same time of conceptual producer, sketch drawer and so on and so forth. He has a massive production team behind him. And in particular two of his closest documenters are close friends who are usually credited in the works in which they participate. And this is something unfortunately I came to think about when I came to the end of my PhD, which is this sense of duplication in the figure of the artist. It is for example Alÿs's walking that makes the practice but also it's Alÿs as documenter that makes his practice live on through documentation. So that's a long answer to it. Sometimes this issue of documentation overtakes Alÿs's work in my mind. And in particular I have the example,

When Faith Moves Mountains, in Lima when he choreographed 500 people and then there's a very telling image in which you see everybody reaching the pinnacle and then there's a helicopter from which there's a massive camera crew taking the entire image. And you see how the helicopter whips sand into the faces of these people who are doing this arduous work of 'convivial building' bla bla bla bullshit in my mind. So there are some works that are more pointed towards documentation. And that particular work, I agree with Santiago Sierra that when he renames it 'When Fairs Move Mountains.'

MH   Is there a sense then that photogeneity determines the – –

AMR   Absolutely. And composition. Old school values of art, so crafting, the materiality, the sensuality of the works of Francis Alÿs, in my mind his hook is aesthetic. You get sucked into it through these very sensuous forms. These very neatly pared-down artworks. There's a lot of craft in giving a semblance of randomness and immediacy but it's actually all very crafted and defined. At least that's my interpretation of it.

VG   Also in the early works?

AMR   Yeah. I'm not sure when this transition particularly starts to happen but, for example, as I showed, *Placing Pillows,* there's only two images that survive of that work, one is the close-up of the pillow in the frame and another is Alÿs just walking around the city. So from the very beginning there seems to be someone else involved already in the documentation. It's my argument that role becomes more and more prominent as the projects become more and more spectacular. So the more humble actions – –

MH   It seems then you have a dilemma between what Alex is doing and what Alÿs is doing - either you stand there as the performer or you film someone else doing your work for you, which I guess is what Alex is doing. But the precedence of the artist being there as a filmed performer exists deeply in contemporary art culture, you've got Beuys for example. And it makes you wonder what isn't represented – in the work *I Like America and America Likes Me* we are told he sleeps in a cage with a coyote but, no, he sleeps in the loft upstairs of the gallery space.

AMR   These are well crafted secrets. And in relation to your work (Alex), also, I think there's Tania Bruguera's work and the production of behaviour and the moulding and instrumentalisation of making art as a 'useful practice' — actually tooling people, or retooling them, refunctioning them so that they would understand different places and different positions in society; and in that her work couldn't care less about documentation for example. The documentation of the piece is done by the audience. Other people documenting the work. So I feel there is a way out of this deadlock of either performer or documenter, in perhaps delegating documentation to audiences.

PF   I see it as engineering, a kind of engineering because going back to the tool part and going back to have a look at the different ways, you can use a drawing as a form of transmitting a way of making something, or building tools as a way of making something. In this new kind of situation where everyone collaborates and there are workshops for all, the only real way of engineering a process of making is to actually know how to engineer a process. To come back to the Beuys piece of engineering, I think it's really fascinating that - here's Francis Alÿs and you get a sense that here's this one person and to hear about the engineering process is fascinating. And when I apply that to what we saw of Alex's work I think about how engineering takes place there and the storyboarding and the preplanning of something - it might has to do with documentation itself. It's really interesting to think of Beuys engineering something. And though we get the sense that the person with the camera has an equal voice, it can't always be the case and often those people are excluded, so I find it talks about who's excluded and what's excluded, as you (Mark) said.

AMR   It's not as spontaneous as we'd like to think, it's not as immediate. There's a lot of mediation.

AS   But also what it does to the audience — watching is also very dramatic. For Alÿs walking through the town, pushing a block of ice with no one recording him would've been a very different experience.

AMR   That also comes out through interviews, you get the sense that if the pictures didn't exist this work would've gone unnoticed in the context of the city. Nobody stops, and he's just a weirdo like any other weirdo. But now we consider this to be something else, precisely through his own documentation.

AS But he might've been a more approachable weirdo had someone not been filming him.

AMR I think that's true too. And not signaling the fact that something was happening through the camera, because it frames interpretation.

VG But maybe there's also the question, in what way is Alÿs's work an urban analysis, an urban study? And compared to yours (Alex), an educational study?

AMR Well I think there are always ethnographic elements to his practice. Usually on the periphery and the backdrop, for example, in the images of the ice melting it's the focus on him pushing the ice but there is background.

VG Place and environment.

AMR Yes tangentially it gives you a picture of place and a picture of site and demographic absolutely but sometimes not necessarily directly. Which I think is also – that's nice, to get a sense of a place obliquely, through different perspectives instead of this macro, mapped out view.

VG To me his work is very much about city. Especially the projects he did in London. And all the control mechanisms in the city.

AMR Absolutely. His background is urbanism and – we're giving back the author function to his practice – so I won't talk about it. [laughter]

PF André Cadere is quite an interesting artist in relation to all this. It could be argued that none of this would've happened had he not pissed off so many people or walked as many places. And I wondered if that was someone you'd linked to historically?

AMR No. Historically what I tried to do was reevaluate, particularly at the beginning, Alÿs's practice against Situationist readings. There's been a lot of literature that points to his walks as being little dérive-like things and I just think that's bullshit. Instruction in Alÿs's work hasn't anything to do with the Situationist International. His works are not instructive. They're not commandments for other people to do. They're descriptions of actions that he's done. And that's really my argument.

AB   I hate to interrupt, but it's five past 5 so maybe this is a good place to end. I think it's interesting that we haven't really been talking about tools as objects, we're more talking about tools as people, maybe the most interesting tools are people. Thank you all so much for coming. Thanks to the speakers and everyone for giving up your afternoon. And to Claire and Flat Time House.

PROTO-TOOLS DISPLAY

Proto-tools Display presents new works by Jonathan Kemp, Colm Lally and Fay Nicolson. The works are installed in the 'Mind' space at Flat Time House along with the permanent exhibition of work by John Latham.

WORK WITH MATERIAL / Heavy Handed, 2013.
Printed text, glazed ceramic. Fay Nicolson.

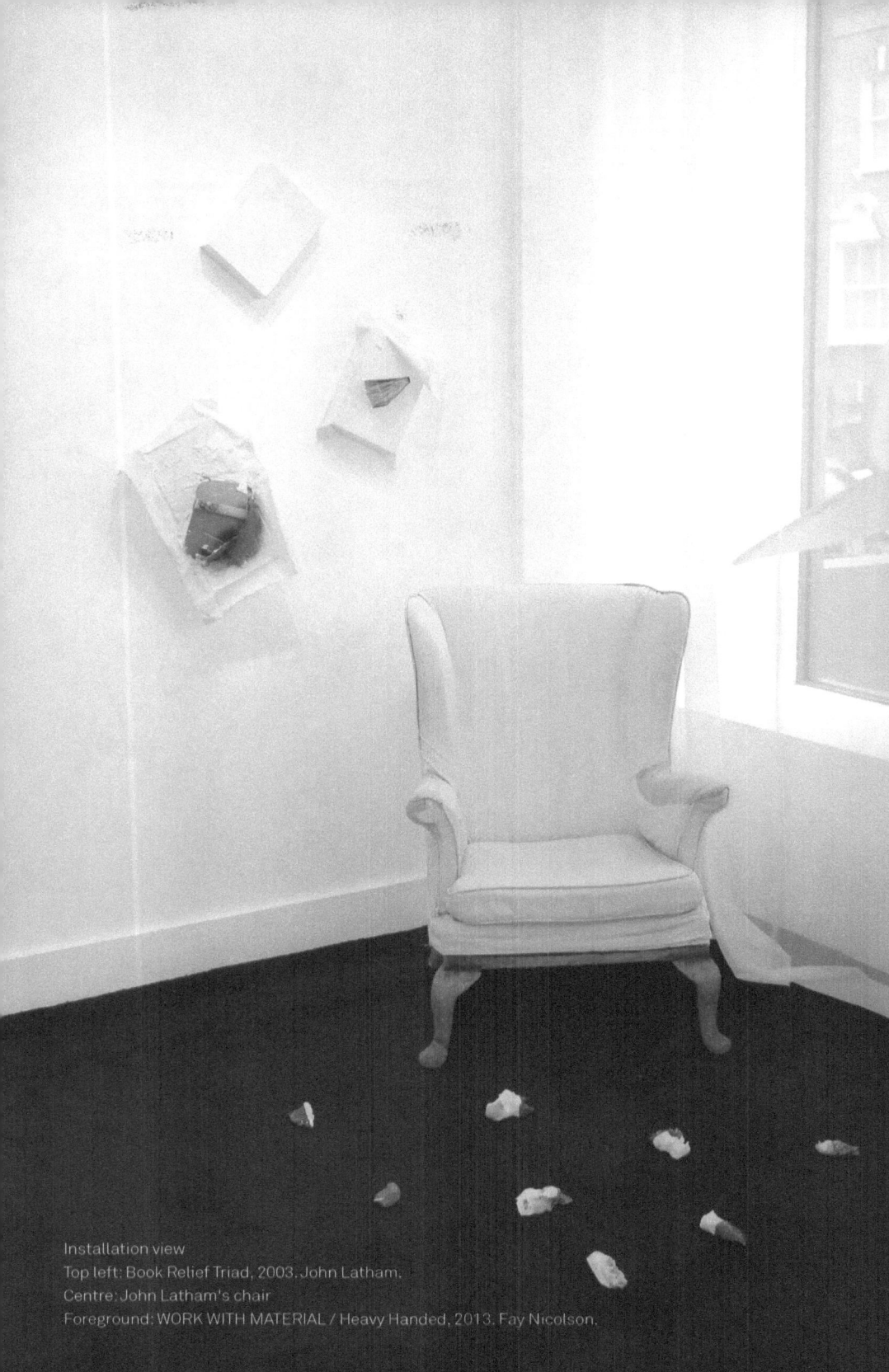

Installation view
Top left: Book Relief Triad, 2003. John Latham.
Centre: John Latham's chair
Foreground: WORK WITH MATERIAL / Heavy Handed, 2013. Fay Nicolson.

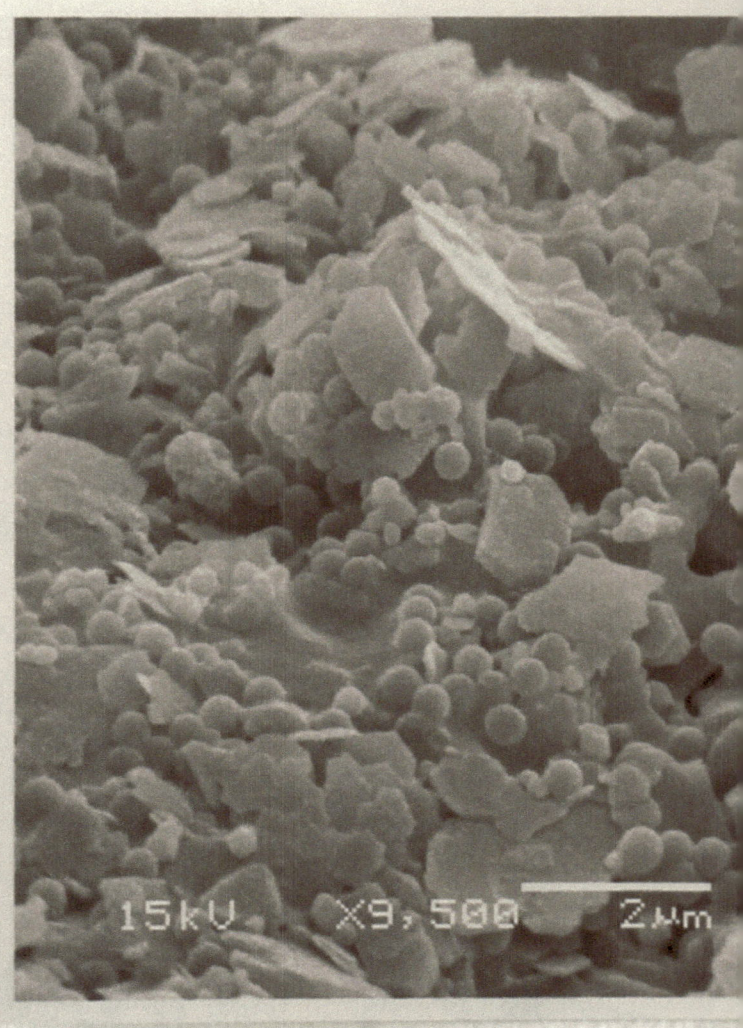

SEM Scan of Flat Time House Wall, 2013.
C-type print. Colm Lally.

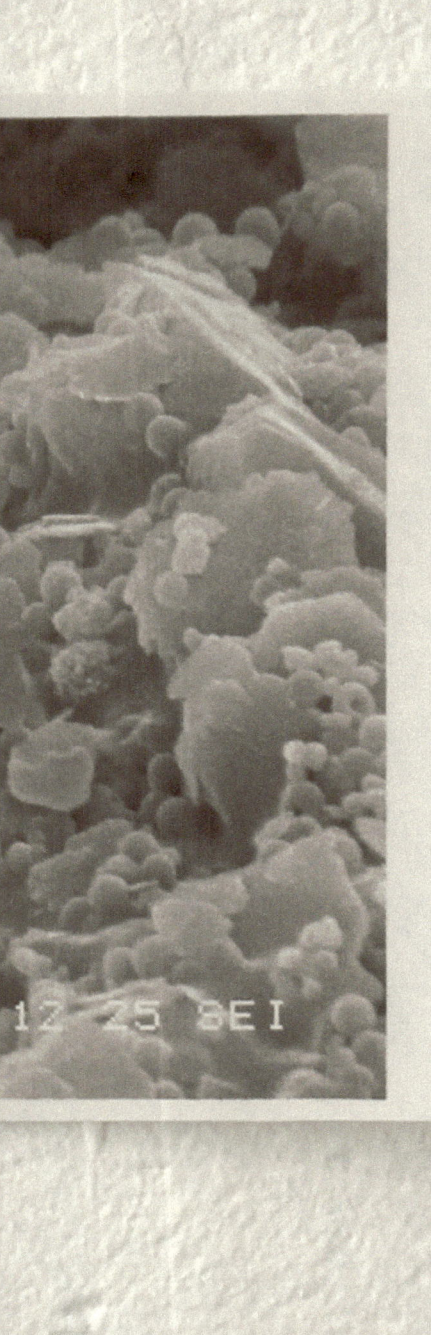

12 25 SEI

Due to a motorbike accident Jonathan Kemp has had to cancel his Silicon Earth performance. Instead he has written the following discription of what he would've done.

Silicon Earth
Performance by Jonathan Kemp, 2013

Simulating the production cycle of silicon, the iconic basis of all computers, my performance-presentation would have used the garden at FTHo to extract and purify a non-natural silicon, reconfigure it, and finally re-enter it back into the earth as an alien geology (anthropocene).

Taking some sandy soil from FTHo, silicon would have been released in its pure form following a simple explosive reaction and subsequent decanting into acid.

The powdered silicon would then have been melted into tiny 'chips' by getting a hacked domestic microwave oven to work at over 1410°C (in a move towards a dirty silicon chip).

Finally, copper electrodes would have been stuck into the ground in the garden of FTHo, and a mini-trench of FTHo soil and crushed silicon chips were to be subjected to a colossal electrostatic HV discharge to fuse as proto-geological forms, presented for further analysis and investigation.

Notes:
— Silicon is the 8th most abundant element but doesn't exist in nature in a pure form (always bound to something else)
— Here it's used as emblematic of the anthropocene (the effect of human activities taken to form the next geological layer) because it underwrites all computers which in turn underwrite nearly all of contemporary activity
— The presentation was a short circuit to stimulate discussion about the relation of the earth to computation

A M P Q R U Z

Time-Base Roller with Graphic Score, 1987.
Canvas, electric motor operating
metal bar, wood, graphite. John Latham.

DAY 2:
PROTO-TOOLS
ARTISTS CONVERSATIONS

SUBMITTED TEXT

INTRODUCTION: THE ARTIST AND THE MATERIALITY OF TOOLING
STEPHEN KNOTT

Tools are vital. Deconstruct the work of any artist and you find that alongside the base material of a work and the context of its presentation and reception, the artist's relationship with the tool is at the fore.

As a specialist in the history of hobbies and amateur craft my interest in tools and tooling, is very much linked to their accessibility. During my PhD on this subject I looked into the history of various tools whose availability and accessibility we now take for granted. Well-known tools such as the pencil, the paintbrush, or paint, all have a history of their own: from being inaccessible things, often produced and sold by specialist firms or workshops within a strictly regulated economy, to their ultimate ubiquity today, filling the endless shelves of a Hobbycraft store [see for example, Henry Petroski, *The Pencil: A History of Design and Circumstance* (1990); James Ayres, *The Artist's Craft: A History of Tools, Techniques and Materials* (1985); and Thierry de Duve, 'The Readymade and the Tube of Paint' *Artforum* (April 1986)].

Access to tools often has an emancipatory quality. With access to a power tool, the 1950s American homeowner no longer had to rely on the handyman, builder or decorator, but could do many of the jobs himself. Being able to purchase paintboxes of watercolour paint in the late eighteenth and early nineteenth century from firms such as Reeves and Winsor & Newton, endowed middle class European tourists with the ability to capture the picturesque scenes they witnessed as a part of their travels on the grand tour. All the tools needed to make a painting were contained within the box, including the paintbrush, blocks of colour, and often porcelain tablets where you could mix colours. Even for women objectified and subjugated in the long history of male patriarchy in the West, access to the tools of embroidery facilitated varying degrees of subjective expression [see Rozsika Parker, *The Subversive Stitch* (1983)].

But what does this all mean for the artist – where does the tool fit into an artist's practice? Answers to this question might tend to coalesce around two oppositional nodes: the tool is either used in a functional manner, or is itself subject to artistic work, perhaps mistreated, manipulated, or put forward as a work of art in its own right. Yet my focus on amateur craft practice prompts me to ask a different question, in particular, how the accessibility of tools affects the artists' attitude to them and their use of them.

It seems to me that much of the canon of Western modern art can be framed and understood through the lens of increasing tool accessibility. The ability for anyone to wield the power of a paintbrush or pencil coincides with the consideration of tools as problems within the artistic process. In modern artistic practice (from the late nineteenth century to the present) tools are key: they break free from the invisibility of function and the expectation that they are merely a 'means to an end'. In the deregulated free market – with no guilds or governing bodies monitoring access to tools – the artists' use of tools becomes a key part of the artistic process. How does the artist distinguish his or her particular approach to tools against the increasingly able amateur who can often demonstrate exceptional mastery of the same processes that were previously the preserve of the artist?

A cursory overview of twentieth century art reveals a number of different ways in which the tool has been radically extricated from its association with function and toyed with as a concept or as a channel in which to reinvigorate artistic practice. These could be tentatively grouped as follows: the tool as the star of the work (exposure); the tool as co-author; imposing limitations or rules on working with a tool or set of tools; re-tooling; and hacking tools.

The Tool as the Star
In 1916, as a part of his exploration of the idea of the readymade, Marcel Duchamp and his friend Jean Crotti bought an ordinary snow shovel from a US hardware store that was then hung up in their studio and photographed [see Calvin Tomkins, 'The Art World: Duchamp and New York Late-night Salons, Studio Sessions, Snow-shovel Buying, and Other Activities of the City's First Avant-Garde' *The New Yorker* (November 1996)]. Entitled *In advance of a broken arm,* the snow shovel is the most tool-like member of Duchamp's readymade family (that included the hat-rack, urinal and bicycle wheel amongst other things), in that it could effect palpable material change through its use: in this case removing snow from pathways and roads.

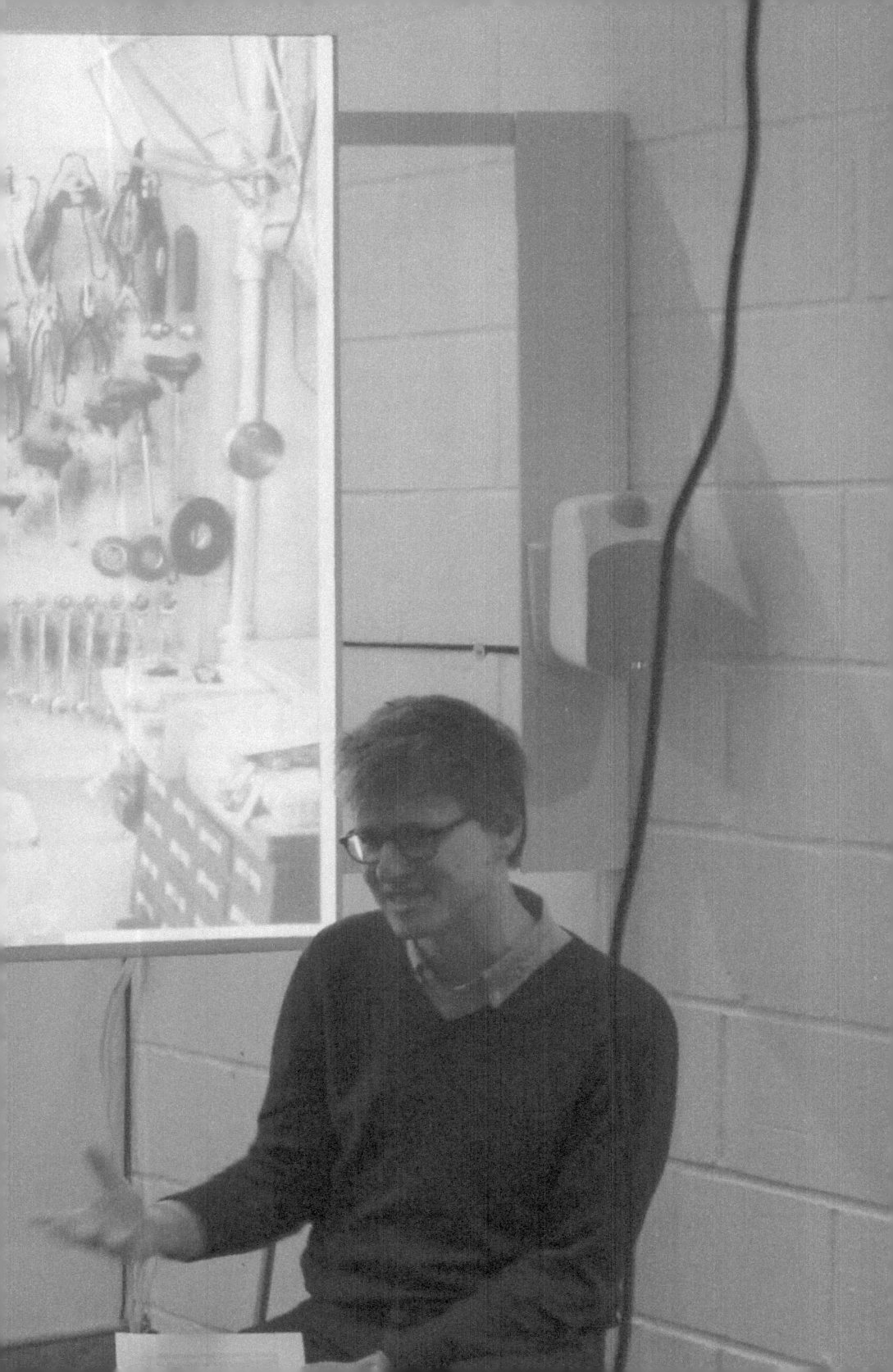

With Duchamp's snow shovel we see the radical and unexpected elevation of the tool as the star of the artwork. With his treatment of the snow shovel Duchamp extracted the tool from its position in everyday routines of use, storage and, to a great extent, invisibility. This was not just a joke, or a stunt by Duchamp to stretch the definitions of what art could be, but was also a celebration of the tool and, by association, the sophistication of a system of industrial production which could produce so many of these tools at an affordable price to help people negotiate the perils of winter. This fascination with the tool was evident in Crotti's treatment of the snow shovel that he was purported to have 'slung the shovel like a rifle over his shoulder' after the duo had bought from a hardware store [see *The New Yorker* (November 1996)]. The snow shovel was worthy of being the star, and exposed to the same appreciation as any other work of art in any of New York's galleries.

Art historian Ezra Shales has developed a reading of Duchamp's readymade that draws attention to the contexts of industrial production of the time, where a snow shovel or a urinal was subject to a certain degree of celebration. He explains in an article in *The Journal of Modern Craft* how subjecting the urinal *(Fountain)* to aesthetic contemplation, through the submission to the Armory Show in 1917, needs to be seen alongside the 'commercial context' where white sanitary ware was considered both hygienic and luxurious; not a ubiquitous commodity, but something the firms who produced them wanted to show off through elaborate retail displays (similar to the plinth environment of the museum) [Ezra Shales, "Mass Production as Academic Imaginary (or if more must be said of Marcel, 'Evacuating Duchampian Conjecture in the Age of Recursive Scholarship')" *The Journal of Modern Craft* 6.3 (November 2013)].

Duchamp's snow shovel demonstrates a radical new understanding of the tool within the artistic process. Instead of being invisible, it is put on full show. The snow shovel could still function, but it is also projected as a final piece of work with a bombastic presence.

This visibility of the tool in artwork can be identified in other moments of Western art history. Before Duchamp, in nineteenth century French impressionism, the tool was obvious in the way the sketch (esquisse) was presented as the final artwork. Impressionist paintings not only depicted landscapes and scenes from everyday life, but the gestural marks of 'en plein air' style through the thick application of paint in tubes that were invented in 1841 for British paint company Winsor & Newton by American John Rand.

Although the artwork had not reached the extent of conceptualism evident in Duchamp's readymade, we could argue that in French impressionism the tool experienced its birth as a self-conscious part of the artwork.

After Duchamp the tool became increasingly exposed in a number of different artistic contexts. For example, in 1960 Jasper Johns produced the *DIY Target,* an outline drawing of a target with pots of paints and a brush attached so that the viewer could imagine finishing the work off, with a signature line that read *Target 1960 Jasper Johns and* _____. The tools here that go into completing the work are exposed in a bombastic manner like a paint-by-number painting, emphasising both John's reliance on the viewer and the importance of the tool's role as co-author, [for more on paint-by-number see Stephen Knott, 'A Theory of the Paint-by-number Surface' in Adamson and Kelly (eds.) *Surface Tensions: Surface, Finish and the Meaning of Objects* (2013)].

With these examples we can see how the tool is re-positioned as an exposed part of the artwork, no longer subservient to the artist's hand. The snow shovel, the tube of paint, Johns' paint-by-number target, all reference the sophistication of modern technology and how accessible tools are in everyday life. One consequence of this is that the authorial voice of artist (particularly the case with Duchamp) becomes increasingly muted.

Tool as Co-Author
The emergence of the tool as the star of an artwork might be seen as relatively rare compared to the much broader phenomenon of the tool as co-author. This relates to the idea that the tool becomes increasingly conceived of as co-author in the production of art, rather than as something to hide.

This conceptualisation of tools as co-authors is increasingly evident in contexts of Russian constructivism and is evident in the film *Man With a Movie Camera* (1929) by Dsiga Vertov. In the film the camera is the co-author in the work's production, not only as the invisible machine that makes the film possible, but also as part of the cast in the film itself. There a memorable moment towards the end of the film where the camera and its tripod magically start to move on their own accord, through the use of stop-frame animation: the tripod walks towards the camera case, from which the movie camera appears and mounts the tripod to perform a variety of different functions/tricks. In this film the tool is represented as a part of a new socialist filmic reality – tool and man come together to create new angles on everyday that are quite distinct from the traditions of narrative cinema in Hollywood, for example. In thinking about the political potential of elevating to tool to position of co-author, we are, of course, reliant on the work of Walter Benjamin and his famous essay *The Work of Art in the Age of Mechanical Reproduction* [in *Illuminations* (1999)].

Works of contemporary art that elevate the tool as co-author also expose issues relating to the social reality of paradigms of production. For example Zoe Sheehan Smith's *Strike Anywhere* match (2007-8) and accompanying assembly instructions published in The Journal of Modern Craft in July 2012 reveal the baffling complexity that goes into the production of even the most ubiquitous of everyday objects [see Zoë Sheehan Saldaña, 'How to Make a Strike-Anywhere Match' *The Journal of Modern Craft 5.2* (July 2012)]. Similarly, Thomas Thwaites' *Toaster Project* (2009-2010), recently acquired by the Victoria and Albert Museum through its Design Fund [http://www.vam.ac.uk/b/blog/network/design-fund-benefit-va-2013-acquisitions (accessed 31 December 2013)], exposes the tool as co-author. But in this instance the tool in question, a regular budget range toaster from Argos that costs £3.49, is shown to have a complex back-story, with materials used for its constructions sourced from around the world. In the course of trying to re-construct this toaster from scratch, Thwaites takes apart the tool to figure out its various components, tries to source the material in Britain (which he finds very difficult given the decline of mining in this country), and re-form this material into the streamlined plastic toaster [see Thomas Thwaites, *The Toaster Project: or A Heroic Attempt to Build a Simple Electronic Appliance from Scratch* (2011)]. In the course of showing the incredible complexity behind the simplest of tools, Thwaites shows how the tool is a co-author with substantial depth that is worthy of exploration. By charting the toaster's origins Thwaites reveals the complexity of modern industrial production, the decline of Britain as a producer of raw material and the social and cultural implications of such changes.

Imposing Limitations or Rules on Working with Tools
Another interesting artistic approach to the ubiquity of tooling and the accessibility of tools is to impose some kind of rule, game, limitation or regulation on the way the tool is being used. In many respects this imposition of a tool order was anticipated by Duchamp who had to regulate and set impositions of his production of readymades, as soon as they started to gain notoriety, otherwise everything in the tangible universe would be a

readymade. For Duchamp this meant regulating the number of readymades he produced in his career (no more than two a year), but for contemporary artists an imposition on how a tool might be used generates an automatic brief and a productive limitation that is useful in an era where artistic practice seems limitless and bereft of borders.

One example of the imposition of a tool order was witnessed in the exhibition at the Milwaukee Art Museum in 2011-12, *The Tool at Hand,* curated by Ethan Lasser. The brief, set to a group of international artists, was to create a work of art using only one tool with a process video demonstrating how the artist approached the brief. Participating UK artist Nicola Probert took apart her usual tool of choice – a video camera – with a small screwdriver. In a piece of auto-destruction, the use of just one small tool allowed the artist to expose the technology behind her video camera, the strewn carcass of the camera finally unable to film itself when Probert severs to the link to the battery.

In the same exhibition Beth Lipman used a caulk gun to glue together objects from her studio to create unwieldy globular sculptures, furniture designer David Gates struggled to work with a reduced set of tools in his discipline that usually requires so many, and Michael Eden showed how much he relied on his Apple computer in the production of 3D printed vessels, with an added subtle acknowledgment of the continuity of tactility in the digital world expressed through his explanation of the mouse-screen-eye interaction.

In a similar vein, the project *Bodging Milano* (2010-present) also imposed a tool limitation. However, instead of requiring participants to only use one tool, the impetus behind Bodging Milano, was to swap an entire environment of tooling with another. In the project a group of London-based furniture designers were asked to leave behind the technological mastery of their well-equipped studios for one week to both learn and master the techniques of greenwood woodworking [see http://www.bodgingmilano.co.uk/ (accessed 31 December 2013) and http://journalofmoderncraft.com/articles/bodging-milano-by-stephen-knott (accessed 31 December 2013)]. Deep in the Herefordshire countryside the ten designers had to battle the cold to both cut down, shape and carve the wood into chairs, following centuries-long traditions of itinerant vernacular furniture makers who made their work by hand. The chairs produced by the group of designers that included Gareth

Neal, Carl Clerkin, Chris Eckersley and Rory Dodd, were shipped away to a furniture show in Milan soon after their week-long course ended. The most relevant conclusion, however, in relation to the subject of this introductory text is how all the designers acknowledged how changing their tool environment reinvigorated their practice by forcing a greater appreciation of the tools with which they are normally surrounded and by encouraging their appreciation of both the difficulty and design potential of hand-powered procedures of working with greenwood.

Hacking

The final artistic approach to tools is to modify, construct or encourage the misuse of tools, to disrupt the passage of a tool's normal function. Analogous to hacking a computer programme, or encouraging a glitch, or cheating in a computer game, this strand of artistic relation to the tool reflects a deliberately subversive attitude to tool function. Multiple examples in contemporary digital culture – such as IKEA hacker, Hackspace, and the explosion in 3D printing technology – reflect both the ubiquity and sophistication of tools, as well as their inherent ability to be subverted or modified to fulfill a certain function (or non-function) by the user in question.

One recent project that delves into the arena of hacking was Xavier Antin's Royal College of Art project for the final graduate show (June 2010) *Printing at Home* [http://www.xavierantin.fr/archive/Printing-at-Home/ (accessed 31 December 2013)]. In the work, Antin modified a standard inkjet printer in a number of different ways that ranged from the humorous – such as attaching printing brushes to the printer head to produce rough large lines of black – to the destructive – such as introducing acid as the printing agent. In the work the printer is modified to encourage a number of visual results that differ from the usual efficiency that is demanded of a printer. In an everyday context you do not want your printer to auto-destruct, but in an era of tool ubiquity Antin, as a critical observer generates a productive revelation of the dynamics of tooling and their potential agency by exposing what interest, chaos or joy a modified tool can produce.

In all these examples the artist or artists place the tool, and tooling centre stage. They all challenge the notion of the tool's subjugation to function, a helpful revelation in an era of the ubiquity of tools, where function and efficiency is often trumped as the prime motivating factor in the tool-human relationship. As the Proto-tools project demonstrates artists, designers and craftsmen have a large role to play in complicating the everyday understanding of what tools mean, their history, and how they are implicated in social and cultural change. This is because they have long problematised the simple presumption that tools are subservient to other narratives.

GIBSON/MARTELLI
IN DISCUSSION WITH COLM LALLY

BM   Do you have a question?

CL   Yes, can you tell me something about the tools you use in your practice?

BM   Ok, well we're Gibson/Martelli. We've worked together for about 10 years. Previously we've been doing a lot of work with computer game engines. I guess, following on from what Stephen said, finally the means of production to make computer games became available to us and we could actually do it at home. We're very interested in figure and landscape. And we come from a background where I guess when we started working together we used to do a lot of performances and we're always really interested in performers and working with them in some way and we're just really interested in landscapes and I guess it's just really old fashioned and pastoral – so I've only got one picture of an old piece that we did and then I've got three or 4 different tools that we used recently when we did a residency in Canada and we thought that would be the best thing to show.

So this is a piece we did called *Vermilion Lake* which was from an exhibition we called *Visitor* – this is basically one of our computer game engine pieces. And just to describe it really quickly – we made a house which is a model of a virtual model of a Canadian cabin. Inside the cabin there was a boat and that acted as an interface so a visitor could sit in the boat and row around a virtual environment which is made using a computer game engine. And you use the boat very naturalistically to row around the environment. With the computer game engine stuff the world is only created when the virtual camera is looking at it. It's like a continuous camera shot where nothing that you're not looking at exists and it gets drawn as you move the boat around the environment.

Then this year we were on a residency again in Canada with CAFKA at Christie Digital, who make a lot of cinema film projectors. And one of the things they have and one of the main reasons we wanted a residency is they have a CAVE (CAVE Automatic Virtual Environment) – it's a recursive acronym. This is technology that's been around I guess from the 90's but recently they've really managed to step up and get the horse-power on it going. So what happens is there's like a square room, missing one wall with loads of projectors and basically you go in and it's all back projected. And they've got 12 stereo projectors, really high-end, high-resolution projectors. And you wear these glasses. They're shutter glasses like when you go to see a 3d film at the cinema and you get a stereo image. And it also has little cameras and these cameras track these balls here using infrared. And they change the view point of the virtual environment you're viewing on the walls so wherever you look you get this perfect 3d view of the world. And the nice thing is because it's tracking your head, if you duck down, if you bend your knees, your view point changes, so if you have a virtual table you can walk round it and you can duck underneath. And this lantern we'll come back and talk about in a minute. You've got like a thing, like a hairdryer that you hold and it also gets tracked and it's like a space navigator that enables you to move around in the virtual environment.

So now I'm going to show you some experimental stuff that we did. So here's a cabin which is in the arctic, in Svalbard.

RG Everything your seeing is a work in progress – and we don't normally show work in progress.

> [video projection: https://vimeo.com/81194026
> and https://vimeo.com/81194025]

BM So we thought let's make a virtual version of the cabin. So the size of the cabin is approximately the same size as the inside of the CAVE. And then we got Dustin to check out the CAVE. Now this is a bit weird because this view point – I'm holding the camera and I've got the magic glasses so it's all from my view point, so everything he sees is really distorted, it's all bent up the walls. So he does a lot of improv. performance, so we thought, lets see what happens when we get a real person inside this virtual environment. So the viewer, in this case me, can get this weird thing that's happening on two different levels. So I'm telling him where stuff is in this 3d world. Because he can just see a bunch of lines – it doesn't make any sense at all to him.

RG   He is super rare as well because he's actually a programmer who is a performer who does improvised comedy. And he worked on the *Kinect Fusion* project so it was really amazing for us to work with him technically, plus having his physicality as a tool.

BM   So now I've messed up and turned the camera around. So now I have to go to another film. So I'm trying to tell him there's the lantern over there because he can't see it. He just sees some abstract lines. After he's practiced for a bit he started to get it. So we were trying to think about that we'd have a performer and get them to interact with the virtual space. And they'd have objects, like maybe he'd take of his coat and hang it up and his coat would just fall on the floor in real life but we'd have a virtual coat that would appear on the wall.

      So here's another tool. This is a tool that's really difficult to get your hands on, called Motion Capture. And this particular motion capture studio is in Australia and it's in a big old theatre space – basically motion capture is a tool which is used by animators and filmmakers for doing CGI special effects. What happens is the performer on the left over here wears these shiny balls. They're retro-reflective markers, like on council hi-viz jackets. And a whole bunch of cameras around the room put the image that they get from each of the balls back together into a 3d file and then you can use it to do animation with.

RG   I'm coaching Wendy in preparation for recording a take. We're interested in this because of performance and you can get some really nice and subtle effects when you are motion capturing because it records at a very high frame-rate and it's sensitive enough, it's millimetrically precise, so for example you can see people breathing even if they're being absolutely still.

      And we thought because we've got a lot of motion capture files from some of our other projects we thought lets try and put it into the CAVE so we have a virtual character that's animated.

      [video projection: https://vimeo.com/81194021]

BM   And Ruth's in there and she's got the magic glasses on and so everything is basically what she is seeing – so we're seeing it slightly distorted.

RG   I'm playing with Wendy's material. You could live stream it too if you really wanted to. My background is in dance so it's extraordinary to be wearing the goggles, it's like deep sea diving but with this other dancer. So at the moment we're thinking about how to work with this for visitors and audiences. And at the moment we're having to strip things down to the very minimum – –

CL   Can the other performer see you?

RG   No.

BM   This is a prerecorded file we're streaming in from another computer. The reason it's moving around is, the performer is actually moving around in space and the origin of the performers movement is aligned with the origin of the CAVE space and so as Ruth moves around the view point shifts to be correct for her. The reason we can see all those balls, it's all doubled up, is because it's a mono recording of a stereo viewpoint.

CL   I have another question – –

RG   Ask us later – because it might make sense later on.

BM   One of the other things we did was when we were in the virtual space it's hard to get shit into the computer and then get it into the CAVE and so one of the first things we did, we made this compass on the floor so you can check when your orientation changes – weirdly the CAVE is like a room you're moving through virtual space, so when she spins the view around the compass changes and we found that was a really useful widget to have to help us orientate, because what happens is you do all this stuff, you programme these things, you don't know how it's going to work, you run it, and then it's just black – –

RG   And there's another beautiful way that you can experiment which is you can take the goggles off and swing them and catch them. Because it's just positional.

[video projection: https://vimeo.com/81194023]

BM   So here's another thing we experimented with – we had a hut, so it's a wireframe hut and we thought it'd also be nice to have a light – lets make a virtual light – so we made a virtual light which is basically a junk shop old lantern that we put markers on so it was trackable. It basically casts a light into the virtual space and you can move the light around. The next stage of experimentation we were working on with Dustin was to use the Kinect cameras, to track people in the space and then use the virtual light to cast shadows. So we got that working but we can't show it to you because we don't have a video.

One of the problems with this is that we had this wonderful opportunity to experiment but then we were thinking 'ok how are you going to show the shit to anybody else?' – it's really difficult, there are some CAVEs in the UK, mostly in universities and it's hard to get access to them. Also their configurations are slightly different, this one is running off 13 PC's but some of them have 6 PC's and then you have to reconfigure everything.

Here's another slide. In the arctic – obviously we're very interested in landscape so we thought lets make some landscape for the CAVE because that's what CAVEs do really well.

RG   I was really into string art when we got to do the residency and we realised the expectations were that we would be expected to work digitally so my obsession with string art wasn't going to go down too well with everyone. So we ended up making the cabin you saw before.

[video projection: https://vimeo.com/81194020]

BM   So we started making landscapes using what is known as height-map data – which is a cartographic process where you measure terrain elevations for map-making and you can turn them into 3d meshes and put them into the CAVE and then you can navigate around. And these are panoramic photographs around the CAVE and I think there's a little video somewhere. So Carl has got the magic glasses, because he's lying on the floor everything has got the right perspective for him but it will all look messed up for us – what we are trying to do is give people these different experiences they wouldn't have normally – the CAVE is great for that because it's this immersive experience, people do all these weird things, rolling around on the floor – –

AB   Times up!

VERBATIM TRANSCRIPTION

JULIKA GITTNER
IN DISCUSSION WITH GIBSON/MARTELLI

BM   So can you talk about your favourite tool?

JG   My favourite tool is not here, it's a really old glue gun that I use for everything, in my art and in my house and everything – I probably shouldn't say that because it's a really crap tool but I love crap tools.

I was going to talk about my work in a sense of using sculpture as a tool which is I think the central aspect of it. And there are 2 sides to it – it's using sculpture as a tool and then it's using sculpture as an anti-tool. I never really thought about it in those terms but thinking about what to talk about today made me come up with that definition.

So in a way I make objects that are not really objects by themselves. I don't just make a sculpture and put it in the space and that's that. The objects are there to set off a process and the process is really the work and that's what I'm really interested in. So I'm just going to show you a few examples and I'm not probably going to show you the whole project each time but I'll just talk about the toolness of it.

So this is a series of sculptures I've made called *Vandals*. And basically they are designed to be vandalised. So they have all sorts of receptacles for things like to be pissed on or for rubbish to be thrown on to them. They are also made to look sturdy. They're made with a fake concrete but actually they're super fragile because I made them with cardboard and paper. So it's sort of a weird piece of furniture that's got a strange functionality to it. So that bit is the tool bit. The idea is that you put this into a public place and it has a sort of function. The function is the thing that people can interact with, because they understand it in a way, or possibly not.

And then throughout all of my work there is always this idea of the anti-tool. And that's to say that it doesn't really quite work, the tool.

So it's a bit crap. And what's really important for my tools is the context they are in. So for instance showing these objects in the gallery space makes the tool defunct – it doesn't really work because no one is going to vandalise a piece of sculpture in a gallery unless you put a big sign saying 'please trash my work' and that's not really the point. So what I do is I put them in places and I chain them to railings. They're on wheels and you're allowed to chain a vehicle in public space

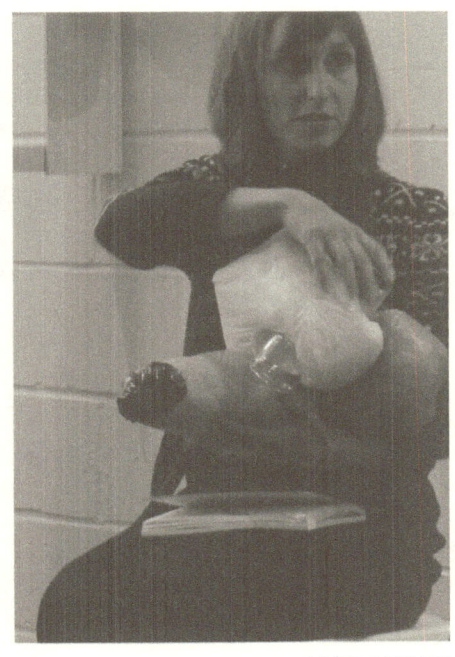

JULIKA GITTNER

without being fined for leaving rubbish, because someone might think this is rubbish. And actually it does turn into rubbish because what happens is basically that the object gets broken, it gets vandalised and in the end it usual gets discarded by the rubbish collection services. So the object is just there to set off that process.

So the other side of making a tool is making objects because I want to understand something. This is kind of the opposite of what you do so I think we'll really well paired. My tools are like the opposite of your tools, they're very sort of simple. But they are also about making something abstract become real and physical, which is obviously quite different to working with making things virtual. So my work is often to do with government policies or rules that we might come across. In this project, from 2011, the time when the government was starting to implement MWRA, which is Mandatory Work Related Activity, as part of the Work for Your Benefit Scheme where they made people do manual labour for nothing – well or for what calculated to be the equivalent of two pence per minute. Which is not a very high wage. So I really wanted to understand what does that mean – so they're making these people work for 2 pence per minute and they're making them do gardening and picking up the litter and community services. So I made these objects – this one is gardening and the one on the left is picking up litter. And I took them to this job centre in Salford. I was collaborating with some people from the Unemployed Workers Union in Salford. We were trying to, in a way, demonstrate or make people experience what does MWRA actually mean. So the object has a button and you press it and it sets off a sound track and that's a one-minute sound track and at the end you've done your one-minute work. I think what is important is that it works and doesn't work at the same time. It kind of relates to your motion tracking because it's based on Frank Gilbreth's early motion studies. He wanted to economise and make workers more efficient so he did exactly what this technology is based on which is to track peoples movements by putting lights on their body and then taking photographs and designing graphs of the movement. So this is where I got the idea of movement as a graph.

So I brought some tools with me here. I'm not going to necessarily talk about what these were part of.. they were part of other work and installations and things. But I guess it's again the question of what a tool should do? So this is a tool, part of an installation of objects that you interact with to pass a test. And the test is the test the government makes people do who want to apply for disability benefit. It assesses their physical and mental capabilities. So one of the questions is 'can you use a keyboard?' or 'Can you pick up a £1 coin?' or ' Can you turn a star-headed sink table? 'Can you touch the top of your head?'. So the installation consisted of all these objects that did materialise that test. But as you can see there would be more efficient ways of making that test 3-dimensional, which is sort of my task. And I think the point for me to include all this stuff around the functional part of the object is to resist this idea of something being functional and that's the sort of 'anti-toolness' of the objects that I make, because I'm against sculpture being instrumentalised, particularly to do with simulating the interference in social issues.

Ok so that's my other tool that I brought. It kind of works. This is called a 'SNACK' and it gets attached to a lamppost with this thing at the back. And it does attach very well to a lamppost and it dispenses government recommended positive life-style choices like '5-a-day', which in this case is only four. And there's another one for non-smoking and so on. So there's this tool to dispense something and it sort of dispenses it but then the question is whether it is a sculpture or what part of it is a tool and what part of it is the sculpture.

And then the last thing I want to show you is where I used in this work which is called 'NGO', or 'Non-Gainful Occupation' (which I think is quite a good description for anything I do as an artist!). The work is based on the Frank Gilbreth's motion study idea of analysing movement, which he used to literally desig every little component of a work movement to make it more efficient. So if I'm packing soap for instance I'm following a particular movement and I can redesign that movement to be more efficient. So I made a sculpture and I filmed myself doing it and used Gilbreth's method and his coding language to then design it in a more efficient way. I think there were 2300 and something movements in me making of this sculpture which took me around 40 minutes, and 900 and something of those movements were inefficient. So I took those out. I made 2 videos of this work. One is 7.5 hours. If you just used the efficient movements to make more objects you could make 19 in a working day, which would be 7.5 hours. So the object is this, it's a pint holder and as you can see it's not a particularly good pint holder. [video]

So in a way, in this one, the object itself becomes a tool for redesigning itself in some way, to become more efficient. And that's the end of what I want to say.

AB   You had 15 seconds to spare.

VERBATIM TRANSCRIPTION

FAY NICOLSON
IN DISCUSSION WITH JULIKA GITTNER

JG   I'm just going to let you speak.

FN   So I haven't done a presentation because I'm quite literal sometimes and I like to look at the brief of things and go back to the beginning and the root of things. So I suppose – and this is part of the way I think about tools in my practice – what I'm doing now might just reflect my working process. I'd like to go back to the text on the website which talks about this event and I was thinking, how do I use tools? And how is that going to be relevant to this event now, and to you as an audience? And there were a few things that were really relevant to me personally, like the interaction between the artist and the object in production, and I was thinking about how production for me is performance. And I thought that was really relevant to you (Julika), and the way that you've recorded your production process and analysed it. And thinking about production and creativity in relation to mass production, and performance, in a way made me think about having to be present to work. Which is also relevant to the idea of working for 2 pence and the current situation that we are all in. And also some of the other ideas, like unknowing. And how far can we extend the definition of the tool? And essentially, how misuse of the tool is a strategy used within the art world, by artists, and why do we do this?

So, starting from the beginning. I'm an artist. I'm unskilled. I cannot and I do not use many tools. I'm not specialised. I use tools badly. I use the simplest tools. I use available tools. And I find the misuse of tools interesting. None of that might be true. But that idea of being unskilled, or de-skilled, the connections between those two terms and the differences between them is something that I've spoken about with lots of people in the past. I studied my MA in the RCA print-making department and because of that structure that I entered into I was always debating with the people on my course, asking are we print makers? Are we anti- print makers? The course starts with a month of going through all the different machines and tools in the department. Learning how to use them so you can then work with them or work against them.

Ok, tools – I think of workmen and craftsmen, they are the first thing that come into mind. So automatically we have this idea of labour and productivity, that maybe out-moded – but also this idea of craft – something that I think Stephen was talking about, with William Morris, was coming to mind – and also, this idea of skill and how it's something kind of dirty. Somebody who can paint really well or use a tool really well, maybe that's something that doesn't have any value in the art world today.

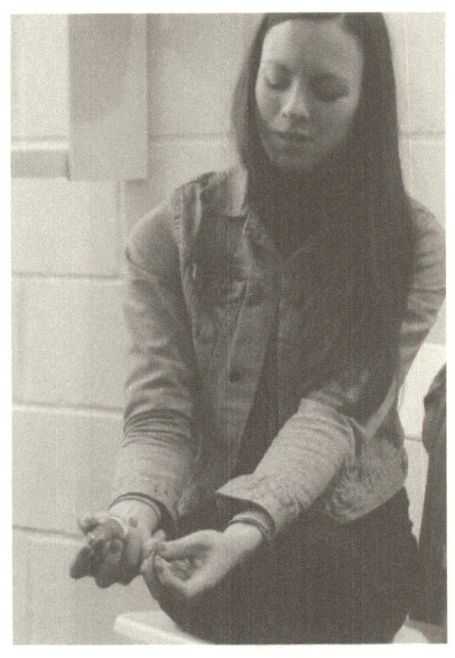

FAY NICOLSON

Tools extend what's possible. Something like a hammer, you put it in your hand and you have this extended reach and a hard edge and just that idea of it being an extension of what's possible. I am also thinking about how, at different historical times, using a tool can make more things possible. But using a tool anachronistically can limit you, so it has the opposite effect. And that in itself has meaning. And I was thinking about tools as mediators. Tools as objects, which I think Stephen mentioned, and then tools as mediators. Tools mediate between an artist, or agent, or person and a process, in the site of production. And then the tool – between the photographer and the photograph you have the camera – what is that mediating process? And how, in industry you might choose the most efficient tool, but within art we want to separate ourselves from the mass-produced object, and so use the least efficient tool. Actually the text talks about the misuse of tools as a strategy against the market's logic of efficiency – but maybe cynically the misuse of tools is a way of saying 'this isn't a mass produced object, actually it's taken a lot of time to do and it's worth a lot of money'.

And I was thinking that I'm really interested in art eduction and learning. So tools within learning. And I was thinking about the first instance of the misuse of a tool is being on a foundation course and someone giving you a pencil and asking you to hold it in your left hand. And at that moment with the simplest of tools and the simplest of tasks, just by misusing it in that way, you are suddenly in a position of not knowing anything any more. You still know everything you did know but suddenly your body – and here's the idea of tacit knowledge – your body used to know how to do things, but suddenly it doesn't. And I'm wondering what the value of that within art education is, as well as why we play these games with knowing and not knowing how to do something?

I don't know, maybe these aren't actually relevant but I've got 3 quotes from a performance I did last year: Josef Albers said, "Recognise the manifold use of material. The changing organisation and presentation unhampered by either harmony or disharmony but lead by a respect for both. If you can do without tools all the better." So this idea of modernist art education of saying, 'lets get rid of the tools, it's all about the hand and your relationship with materials directly. And Anni Albers, who I'm really interested in, said, "Civilization estranges men from materials in their original form. For the process of shaping these is so divided into separate steps that one person is rarely involved in the whole course of manufacture, often knowing only the finished product." And the final one is paraphrased from Carl Goldstein talking about renaissance art academies onwards, "In the advent of the machine, when the hand of the worker (and the skill it represents) becomes obsolete, the art academies come to value the hand. It is summoned and the marks it makes are celebrated as the residues of an almost spiritual instrument."

So, also thinking about how it's marking out its territory between the accessibility of materials in relationship to mass production and the non-artist world and kind of playing a game of how things filter in and out of both worlds. And how it keeps its distance. So maybe the availability of digital tools, when anybody can edit a music video – and that relates to Stephen's discussion of painting kits – how does that effect the way artists use video? And I was thinking about how Ed Atkins uses video and uses technology so artfully, so skilled, but in one of his most recent videos he used a digital filter to put fake hairs in the film so it looked like an authentic kind of analogue film, but he used the filter so much that it became perversely visible as a filter.

I work with analogue images and I have an archive of images, and I'm still working out why I do that. And I don't want to think that it's completely sentimental – my love for analogue. But at the same time I think there is something about the restrictions that are there and the fact that it's a tool that is not about possibility, it's about restrictions – So how much time have we got?

AB   6 minutes

FN   So I'd like to open it out and talk about art eduction and where did you (Julika) study?

JG   I went to Goldsmiths.

FN   And were tools spoken about in that environment? Or were there workshops?

JG   The workshops were almost totally abandoned because people thought it was really uncool to learn something. Maybe that has changed, I don't know. I think also, because I am also an architect, the idea of a tool having to work really well, like a tool which isn't supposed to be aesthetically pleasing necessarily, but is supposed to do the job really efficiently. I think that is something that is very much related to design practice and architectural practice as I've gotten to know it through architecture eduction. I mean I was kind of told off at art school for using crap tools and making everything look crap, but I didn't really come across a training with tools. Whereas you obviously did.

FN   Yeah, well I think it's easy to be anti-skill, anti-craft maybe in art school and I think the RCA is quite old fashioned. But I love the freedom – I was struggling against it in a kind of love/hate relationship with this ridiculous idea of fine art being divided into 4 courses that were structured in terms of discipline. So there's not just fine art like there would be in Goldsmith's, but it's painting, print-making, photography and sculpture. And, apart from the different architectural sites, it's all about the tools. It's all about, you know, in print-making you have the printing presses; in painting actually there are no tools, there's just a big studio and bring your brush and – I don't mean to sound cruel to any of the painters but their studios used to be opposite the cafe, and at night you could kind of sit and watch them over the road and they'd just be sat there looking with their brushes and their paintings – and it was such a different way of making work. And if you go into sculpture there's people in boiler suits carrying really heavy stuff around. Although these are stereotypes there is an element of truth. And I was thinking why on earth we should be teaching 4 different versions of fine art when it's not really relevant to today? I mean everybody is a bit of an expert on everything – and these disciplines aren't relevant in the art market. Galleries don't say, 'this sculptor' they say 'this artist'. But then I realised it gave us this amazing opportunity to have a really, rather than a horizontal knowledge base, a vertical one. So at a time when educational institutions cut facilities – it costs money to have tools and it's easier to have a course without any – I actually found it really liberating. And also what's nice about it is it shifts the emphasis away from language-based learning. And suddenly you can take time to work with material as a tool and I think it offers up an alternative to everything being mediated by language, and words being the starting point and finishing point for all kinds of production.

JG   Is this a tool? [holding a small ceramic object Fay has made]

FN   In a way – I'm a resident artist in a secondary school and for a recent exhibition I had some silk prints and I wanted to weigh them down with something and I was fascinate by the pottery room in the school and how important it is in the way that it determines how art is made – and these objects are handfuls of clay I ripped off and I was thinking about – they look like found tools, but also they're also casts of my hand as a tool. And I think they're quite dumb as well which is why I like them – they're like the simplest thing you could use. But I thought I'd give you one to hold.

JG   Have you decided whether you are a print-maker or not? Is there a point at which you have to decide?

FN   I'm definitely not a print-maker but I've always been really interested in mass production and repetition. And the image in the mass realm and something that can be in-between the art world and the public realm which is why I think I found print-making interesting. And I never know where I stood to painting and sculpture – feeling that it was always a bit detached from the world I existed in. But I think those divisions are broken down in a different way now because of the internet.

AB   Time's up.

VERBATIM TRANSCRIPTION

REHANA ZAMAN
IN DISCUSSION WITH FAY NICOLSON

FN   So we've both been very busy and we've had a couple of email exchanges and we were debating about how to approach this and we weren't sure how.. But you've asked me to ask a few questions about your practice, is that right?

RZ   Yeah, ok.

FN   Is there anything in what I spoke about before the break that you connect with in your practice? Or would you like to start from fresh?

RZ   Maybe it's really useful for me in terms of the things that we've covered – I felt that there's a few ways of talking about work that perhaps I have not entirely identified with. Maybe it's useful to figure out what a tool is? Because for me that is quite a fluid idea. Maybe it's useful to do that because, in terms of a certain way of working that's identified through the painters boxes or things like that, that feels quite different to the way that I work. Or if we're talking about the skills- based learning within a workshop scenario, that also feels quite different because – relating to an approach to art-making that comes from one's education, in this case Goldsmiths – there's another Goldsmiths student here who is pretty unskilled, [laughter] and so me starting off making and my practice being rooted in performance and that being about an economy of means and a desire to use my own body and my own presence within the work and that being the material, that being the tool, initially. And it sort of gaining momentum and becoming more video-based. And yeah, we can talk about skills now that have been accumulated along the way. But when we talk about tools in terms of my own work, is it the camera that's used to record the video or is it the pen or the laptop I'm using to write the script or to research to gather bits of information or Final Cut, or if it's actually a way that I'm working at the moment – at the moment I'm really looking at the process that leads to the production of the video. So quite often I'm working on projects more recently which have a workshop background and so it's kind of setting up a situation or initiating some sort of collaboration or conversation with a group of people as a means to generate something that ends up being a video or an installation or a performance or a text even, in a magazine. So I guess I'm thinking about using the language of the workshop then and that being very much a contemporary way of thinking about tools and it comes from this business of 'immaterial labour' and tools being devices – –

FN   Can I interject there? I was just thinking about the difficulty in defining tools now and thinking about the abstraction of the term tool because of a thing such as 'immaterial labour', for example when I'm teaching or running workshops people say to me things like, 'well you know what you're trying to do is give these kids a tool-kit' – –

RZ   That's exactly what I mean yeah – so for instance one of the projects that I did this year had a year-long workshop process attached to it. And the invitation emerged from a gallery inviting me to collaborate with a group of people. And me thinking that's really strange, you know – why should that be just a given that we would work with people who aren't involved in the arts? And that interrogation being a useful site for production. But then you realise that you are performing these things and using these devices that are tools for learning, and all this kind of stuff but the flip side of that is that it's also embedded in a different kind of economy where it's all about business management culture. And we talk about using other people as tools. And I guess the idea of a tool is kind of very fluid. And when we talk about it in terms of the hammer and the nail, there is a very clear definition between what is the tool and what is the material that is being worked. But when it becomes this sort of nebulous set of relations, then where is the tool being enacted, and where is the material, and where is the work?

FN   That's something I was thinking about and I think it's really interesting as well how you say that you were never concerned with using tools in that way because, you mentioned Goldmsiths, and also you mentioned you work with performance and that maybe it's a dematerialised practice and perhaps situations or contexts and relationships are the mediums that you're working with, which are intangible, I suppose the idea of tangibility and body, does that figure at all?

RZ   What do you mean? Sorry.

FN   I suppose I'm trying to think about material in an open way and the reason I was using clay is I started thinking about connections between the digital and clay, so thinking about the fact that the digital mediates our experience a lot now and there's a lot of artists working with clay, or have returned to it, and is it because it offers this tactility? So is it reactionary to return to a material?

RZ   I think you can think of it like that but then on the other hand the cynic in me is like well, is it a desire to return to a more tangible and more physical object-based relationality? Or is it just the fact that, you know, that ceramics are really cool now and art fairs really love objects and you know people are knocking em out and that's a really 'on-it' thing to be making. The slightly bitchy cynical side of me would say something like that but not to discredit it because there's something really satisfying about suddenly engaging with materials again in this way when our discussions about interactions and that being 'work' and anxieties of living in this digitised weird space of being networked. It's kind of reassuring to have those very real situations, like going for a walk or something, or going for a run is suddenly reactivating your physicality. So I don't know.

FN   In a way I agree with you, but do you think there is an issue – you talk about the saleability of the object, maybe in reaction to a shrinking market and artists need to survive – but do you think that performance is also implicated?

RZ   Well exactly. Sorry I probably wasn't being very clear but that's exactly why I think that the use of performance isn't this emancipatory thing that maybe it was in the 60's, as a step away from the market, because it's so embedded in business culture and we are these multi-taskers that have to be social at work. Those relationships are really important and you go on team-building exercises and the workshop is completely central to that. So in a way for me the desire to really try and interrogate that space is to try and see where this originates from. Looking at the space of theatre and actor's workshops and connecting that with some of the other interests I had in political theatre. But also, that being a space where you can kind of, erm, build these actors games and improvisation games and word association games towards a performance perhaps. Their use is repurposed by being part of business culture now. And again looking at how my use of them to produce artworks is also mis-purposing them because we're doing improvisation games but we're not going to make a play and we're not rehearsing together. This, the process of utilising actor's rehearsal strategies, is actually kind of redundant because we play these games and then somehow a video comes out of that. Perhaps trying to open up a debate on how they are used in society now, or to examine those social relationships.

FN   The people that you work with, are they artists, are they paid? I think you mentioned they are from outside the art world, are they your tools? What's that dynamic and what's your position in that?

RZ   How much time have we? [audience laughs] So it really varies according to the project so there isn't one approach. So for instance I work with a crew quite often – and I say crew but it's like, my friend with a camera, my friend a mic and a bit of lighting maybe and that's a paid relationship where we'll make sure they get paid where possible. And actors will get paid where possible. And if not, then the invitation to work together is based on – they are people I've worked with before or people I know – there's an incentive beyond – so I don't really see them as tools, I find that very dubious to describe a person as my tool.

FN   But do they know what they are entering into?

RZ   If it's professionals then yes of course. And then with this project where I was working with a group of people, no they weren't involved in the art world and they weren't paid but the collaboration was set up by the gallery so I kind of went in as a facilitator.

FN   So you are the tool? You are the mediator?

RZ   I think it doesn't quite work to describe me as a tool. I went in as the workshop leader and the games that we played were the tools and devices – games and activities to set something off in motion. So yes, I was definitely the person going in, in charge with all the knowledge, but there was a gesture there to hand over some control to allow the narrative that we would create together to be generated by them so it was co-authored in terms of whatever we produced. But in terms of my role in that situation I had asked those people to work with me and along the way I think they got some stuff out of it. But then it always changes and I think that's what my interest is as well.

FN   You say workshop but are there aims for the workshop in an educational sense? For example, I want these people to learn these skills and come out of it with some kind of experience or is it a case of you know what you are trying to get for this piece of work whether that's setting up the documentation in a certain way or trying to get them to act in a certain way?

RZ   With this it was not like that. It was more like my interest is this situation – I'm going to go into this situation and whatever comes out of this situation is the work. But – one of the questions I had as well was in relation to you showing the objects with the hand print marks – so what I found the tricky bit is, to what extent that process is translatable? To what extent, if you're not just going to do the readymade, to what extent can you start to talk about those processes and how do you make those tools visible in an interesting way that helps unravel what happened when you applied those tools, so not just literally describing them.

AB   Time's up.

VERBATIM TRANSCRIPTION

NEIL CHAPMAN
IN DISCUSSION WITH REHANA ZAMAN

RZ   So a really simple question to start with.

NC   Oh you're going to give me a question?

RZ   Is that alright?

NC   Yeah.

RZ   I just thought it might be good for you to establish where you see the tools in your practice.

NC   So it would be a series of mundane tools which would be writing implements of one kind or another. So that would be a pencil, a pen but also maybe the old typewriter and the word processor on a computer. And from that maybe printers of various kinds – so the big inkjet printer that I have, A3 printer – that'd be a tool which allows the materialising of what's produced in writing – that I then feed back into the process of writing. So in that sense the paper on which the writing is produced becomes a tool as well because it allows you to have a different relationship to what you might've been producing if you were just working with a keyboard and a screen. So lets say you produce a passage of writing and you send it to print and you come back to it a bit later and your dealing with a different material artefact, which you mark up perhaps, with a pencil perhaps. And so a pencil is a tool. And the writing which you produce in a material form is a tool as well, which gives you a different aspect on what is yours supposedly as an author, a self-authored text that comes across as alien when you see it printed.

RZ   Will you talk a bit more about your writing then and how you see that specifically in terms of what it is you're putting down on paper and how you see that operating as a tool? Or what the relationship to materiality is?

NC   Well I would be in that odd position that maybe quite a lot of artists are in at the moment having had a training in art, gaining a kind of status as an artist on the basis of that training and then realising that the work is somewhere else, so that's the relationship with writing. It's an exit in a sense. It's an interesting exit from art practice. So it's related to art – I don't stop being an artist, but I'm always on the way out of art. And that route out is writing in every case – almost every case, except that

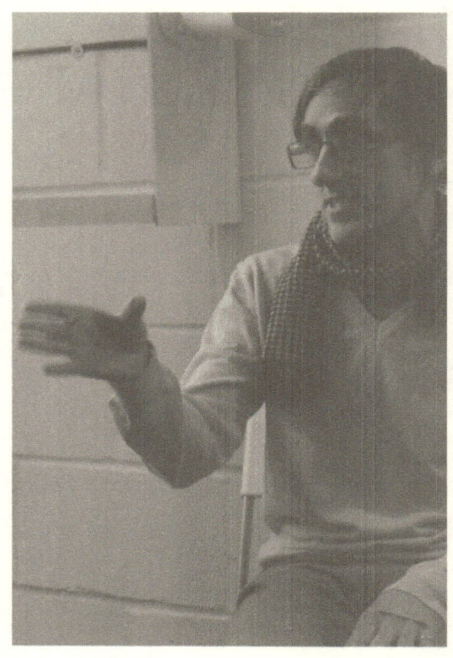

NEIL CHAPMAN

there's a kind of programme as well which involves thinking about how a field, which is mainly writing, might be expanded. So maybe that's something that an artist can do in a way the writer can't.

RZ   When you say writing do you mean – just to be really literal about it – do you mean fiction, do you mean essay writing, or a combination of those things, what exactly do you mean when you say writing?

NC   I suppose it is something a little bit more difficult to pin down than that. It's much more like a mechanics, which is why it's interesting talking about the tools. So in that way it expands what writing might be. It's not defined in terms of categories that would be literary categories in a sense. I mean, what kind of writing – is it fiction or is it something else is already to be in a field of literature – using the terms of literature. It's a bit of a generalisation but to think of writing in that way is already to be kind of figuring yourself in the realm of literature and maybe it's quite interesting not to do that. Maybe that's what happens when artists write, actually the writing can be thought about in a different way. And it can be thought about as a material practice which again is why it's interesting to think about the paper and the actual text as a tool. So the idea there would be to try to expand what writing could be and take that for a moment to be the artists programme – what an artist might contribute. And it's not exactly to contribute to literature because presumably the artist who writes doesn't really care about literature any more than he or she cares about art. So leaving a field of art has got that pejorative feel about it – going somewhere else. Maybe the point here is also not to arrive somewhere either. But certainly not to arrive at literature but to do something, to perform some kind of act on these fields of work.

RZ   When we spoke briefly on the phone you mentioned you were interested in this idea of the misuse of tools.

NC   Did I?

RZ   Well a lot can happen in a week! [laughter]

NC   I've been noticing that that did come up quite a bit already. I think Stephen mentioned it at the beginning and Fay was talking about it.

RZ   So maybe we've covered it – but whether you saw it relevant to your own writing, as not writing literature?

NC   I'd like to think that that is the case but it's always more difficult than you might think to misuse a tool. So for instance there was a period of time a few years back where someone I was working with – two of us were working with an old typewriter and it was the first time I'd come across a Brother electronic typewriter which has this curious quality that when you press a key just a fraction of a second later you get a big clunk. So you press a key and nothing happens and then clunk. And if you're touch-typing that can screw your typing completely. If you are used to hitting the key in the right way. So there's a misuse of the tool there in so far as what that does to your typing and the result can be quite interesting. And so there was a series of documents made using this old typewriter, where what was interesting there was the mistyping. So that was a misuse of the tool – was that a misuse of the tool? I don't know if it is really. But it is kind of because what would be – –

AM   No! [laughter]

RZ   Well in a sense you're using the – the typewriter wouldn't normally be used in relation to producing an artwork, so maybe the artwork is maybe this incoherent writing that you produced through the use of this tool that is supposed to be making writing easier but actually is making it harder. So in a sense it does make a – –

NC   That's the misuse that's taking place. It's not exactly a misuse of the tool. It's almost like – in that situation, if you're to carry on in that vein of making work in that way you have to resist the natural tendency you might have to learn how to use it. So after you've been typing with this old Brother typewriter for a little while and you get the hang of it and that's the end of the work in a sense.

CL   Can I say something to that because I think it's a really good example of where a tool can disrupt your thought pattern – where it actually disturbs you to the point where the delay or the expectation of action and result will be disruptive – which I think is a really effect kind of thing, where, going back to your point that it's difficult to find those examples, where something is really penetratingly changing the conditions of your production, where you're not kind of deliberately doing it.

NC   There's another good example, a canonical example in a way, of the same kind of thing in a book that was recently produced of Robert Walser's micro scripts. Towards the end of his life he was writing on tiny bits of paper, like bus tickets and he was using a really fine point and he was using a version of shorthand which he had invented. It was an amalgamation of various types of scripts that he was producing, something that was only readable to him. And for many years it was thought that they were indecipherable until one of them was printed very large on the front of a magazine and some bright spark somewhere realised that he could read it and he could work out how to decipher it. And these very short stories were produced in a book, so you get the document, which is literally that size, printed on one side of the paper and you get the story on the other side. They're interesting because they're uncorrected proto-stories if you like. And so you learn a lot about the writer when you see the work that's not corrected.

RZ   That leads me to my next question if we've got a bit of time, which is to ask you what you felt the political potential of repurposing or maybe obscuring or interrogating this processes, or inventing obstructions to production? And why would you want to do that in relation to yours?

NC   Well there's at least 2 ways of approaching that. One would be to think about it in terms of disciplines as I was saying before that what's at stake if you're thinking in terms of your identity as a maker, is the relationship one discipline has to another and the stability of one discipline next to another and the propensity that discipline has to change or not. And so the escape from art, the route out of art practice, presumably does something to the realm you left so it's depleted in some kind of way or maybe not depending on who's leaving, and the field that you are approaching – it could be literature, it could be science, lots of people have an art/science trajectory – what happens there is that the boundary – it's a work on the boundary isn't it, it's a shifting of the boundary – you allow the boundary of the discipline to shift in a way – in a way perhaps that writers are not capable of doing in this case.

RZ   Do you see a desire to operate on margins or the boundaries as being an escape from the centre?

NC   Well that's right. That'd be a way of thinking about what the politics of the practice are – but just very briefly the other way of thinking about it, to go back to Walser again, is to think about different terms of the politics of the self as well because his point of writing with a very tiny point and writing on bus tickets was in order to try'n convince himself that he wasn't writing, to fool himself that he wasn't actually writing – arguably that's what he was doing. To forget his expertise. To force himself to forget his expertise. So that is the emergence of a different self or a work on the idea of the self as well, which is also a politics, politics of making. And so those could be two ways of thinking about it perhaps.

RZ   I think it's interesting the way you're – talking about the centre being saturated or potentially depleted – I'm not sure I agree with that – –

NC   No it's interesting in relation to what we were talking about with regard to Dean Kenning who is not hear today – who chose not to come because there was no pay. In one sense the art world is a saturated buyers market. That's why nobody gets paid. There's too many people.

RZ   There's not enough writers so there's more chance of you getting paid?

NC   No, there's no chance of me getting paid.

AB   Time's up.

BM   Can we see your pencil? What size does it become unusable?

NC   Good question, I think I've got another 17mm there.

CL   Is that like a page worth?

NC   I don't know. I do a lot of sharpening. I do more sharpening than I do writing. [laughter]

VERBATIM TRANSCRIPTION

COLM LALLY
IN DISCUSSION WITH NEIL CHAPMAN

NC   So Colm I thought we could try'n have a discussion.

CL   Let's have a discussion. So we haven't prepared anything at all – –

NC   That's fair to say.

CL   That is fair to say. But can I just say one thing to you – –

AB   Is this part of the discussion? Shall I start the timer?

CL   Yeah you might as well start the timer. Can I just say one quick background thing is that we collaborated a bit on this book (*E:vent Archive and Related Material 2003-2011*) – –

NC   It's funny you should mention that because I was going to – –

CL   Ok, shall I just hand it over to you then? Ok, I will then.

NC   Well I was just going to say that – in a moment I was going to talk about that because Colm and I did a little bit of work together – I was commissioned basically or hired for a series of conversations in advance of the book being produced. Which was quite interesting. So we met and we had a series of 2 hour meetings in the Royal Festival Hall and later the book came into being. So you've already kind of prepared in your head to talk about this so you said you hadn't prepared but you have in fact. You know that we're going to talk about this.

CL   Well I was going to ask you can we – only because I actually wasn't going to talk about this but last night I thought that maybe it seemed more appropriate.

NC   So prepare your thoughts because I'm going to ask you some questions.

CL   Please do.

NC   But first of all I wanted to talk about Proto-tools because I thought it would be quite interesting to talk about the title for this event, which nobody has mentioned so far. The fact that this event is not about tools, it's about *Proto-tools*. And what is a Proto-tool? What might that be? So that's what I was thinking about as a beginning. It seemed to be a really interesting idea and it has been quite productive thinking about it this week – so I have actually been preparing because I've been thinking what Proto-tools might mean. And it seemed to me that there were 3, at least, definitions of what that might be. A Proto-tool might be the first tool, the first one. So I was thinking an example might be from Stanley Kubrick's *2001: A Space Odyssey* – that opening sequence where there's an ape with a bone and the bone is thrown into the air and then there's that famous cut where the film goes to this space craft so the bone becomes a space craft – it's a straight cut – a little bit goofy cinematically but it's quite interesting. So that'd be one way of thinking about it. And then there was another idea that occurred to me which is that the Proto-tool might mean a tool for making a tool. That's another possibility so – so that would be the kind of tool that you would use to make a drill bit for instance. And let's just say for arguments sake you want to make a hard steel drill bit, it's a very hard steel that's used for that so you need an even harder steel to make the drill bit. So the material that has to be cut, has to be cut with something harder. And what is that? I don't know, it might be a diamond bit or something like that – –

BM   I thought those tools were called machine tools.

NC   Well the cutting edge on a lathe would be a machine tool but you need a tool to make the machine tool. So for instance that's made of a hardened steel, but you would use a grinder – so here you would use a stone to cut the steel – so anyway these are the less interesting versions of what a Proto-tool might be. There's another one which is a Proto-tool as a shadowy kind of entity or component that is before the tool comes into being – it's the idea that in advance of the tool there is something there – I was going to say it might be the parts that make up the tool – something a little bit like that – we were talking about hammers earlier – so there's the handle and the head I guess... but there's another idea which is invoked here in what comes in advance of the tool which is that a – –

AM   Can I ask something? Does this lead to a question?

CL   This is the way Neil and I converse, he talks and I listen. [laughter]

RG   I find it really interesting.

AM   Yes but maybe it's interesting for a discussion afterwards.

NC   Ok, I'll be really brief. So the other idea is the idea of something that's ready to hand. So you're in your working process, you're in the middle of making something and you realise that something needs to be done and you don't want necessarily to go away and find precisely the right thing for doing the job because that would interrupt the process of the work so instead of going away and finding the thing you stretch out your hand and pick up what's ready to hand. And at that point you're looking for something, it doesn't matter what it is so long as it has certain qualities – let's say you're hammering in a nail; it's got to have a heavy weight; it's got to have a certain number of qualities – those qualities are the Proto-tools – those are the Proto-tools – those are the Proto-tools.

So we had our meeting – we had a series of meetings – we talked. It was open. He (Colm) said let's talk. I'm going to make this book. Let's meet and talk about it. So we had a series of discussions and the book appeared a little time later. But there was a period of time in-between when nothing happened, when the book didn't appear. And it was quite a long time. So what happened in that period of time? And is there some way of talking about – I mean is that where the Proto-tools came into being?

CL   Yeah – I was thinking that a lot of the things that you just said – not the same things – but things around this came up. And one of them was the idea of the prototype – I think actually in a discussion with you the idea of a jig came up as almost like a temporary tool to do a specific thing and it would never really establish itself as a proper tool. But this idea of a Proto-tool could be a tool that doesn't yet know what it is. And then thinking in terms of the practice of art making, this 'pro-flexive' activity which is Marcus Steinweg's idea that in the process of making, artists move between moments of knowing what they are doing and not knowing – or perhaps at times just knowing that the tool is doing something with the material.

But then how that connected to the E:vent book was – actually through our conversations I remember we went through a whole series of possibilities of how to approach archiving the E:vent project and it's funny that we end up in a conversation here today and I didn't even think about this till this minute but one of the ideas that we had, that we came up with at the time – is it over a year ago?

NC A year?

CL 2 years?

NC 5!

CL Two years ago! But one of the things we talked about was that Neil was going to interrogate me and we were going to do it as a performance and he was going to put a spotlight on me in front of an audience and he was going to try and make me remember what happened. Because it just happened that I was there for everything – in probably the same way that Claire is probably here for everything that happens here. So the tool in that case would be my memory, which is actually really really poor so that would've been a really small publication. [laughter]

NC Right but isn't the forgetting – isn't there something crucial about the act of forgetting that conditions the space between the discussion and the production of the object? Is that not what happened? Did you not just forget all the discussions in a purposeful way before you actually came to make your book?

CL Yeah I guess – this came up yesterday, the interview and how it is gaining currency in the art world. And one of the issues with it is where the artist uses it as a self-mythologising mechanism. Where you have the possibility to conveniently remember some things and conveniently forget other things and somehow reposition yourself and reposition what happened. One of the people who spoke yesterday (Verina Gfader) had interviewed (the Italian sociologist and political philosopher) Antonio Negri and I asked her if there was a sense of responsibility to try to make sure history doesn't get rearranged in this kind of interview scenario. Because it's one thing for an artist to use the interview to rearrange what happened – or just to relate it to the E:vent archive, I was talking to an art historian about compiling this archive and I asked her had she any advise and she said that I had an obligation to history to document the titles of the shows, the names of the artists involved and the outline of what happened, beyond interpreting it, just to mark what happened. So although you (Neil) and I began with a whole series of interesting ways of dealing with the archive and dealing with the fact that no matter how you approach compiling an archive, you begin to rewrite what happened. And although we were going to try to address this issue head-on with those experiments I mentioned, I suppose in the time that I forgot those things that we spoke about, in that time, I veered towards making a stab at an objective account.

So in this archive – it is definitely a tool – in the middle of the book is – all of this bit of it is just what happened, as much as you can put down on paper. And at the beginning is an introductory text by Peter Lewis who outlined possible ways into the archive, and at the end is this 'exit' which is – because you (Neil) talked about exiting art earlier, but in a different way the exit from this book is again not to arrive at any conclusions about the contents of the archive. So what we did was, I gave Neil some of my notes about what I had thought the project (E:vent) was about at various points along the way. Some of the notes are dated from the beginning and some of them are dated later on. And some of them are emails that I had written to people about it, describing it for various reasons for various projects. So I gave this to Neil and he wrote a text that just sits along side it. So that's how it ended up as a format.

NC   You've skated over something quite interesting there in suggesting somehow that you've done something quite straightforward with the archive which is just to represent it, but actually that's not the case. The way that it's presented, it's quite important the way the actual material gets presented in the book. You've made a whole series of decisions about how these events are documented.

AB   I'm afraid your time is up.

OPEN FLOOR DISCUSSION

AB   We have 15 minutes to open it up for questions. So anyone can ask anyone a question.

CL   I have a question for Ruth and Bruno – it strikes me that you have such a broad range of influences that you bring to your practice and this very broad range of sensibilities with regard to the various tools that you use, like very broad it strikes me, more broad than most artists. And I was wondering because you've got all of these concerns that you carry with you from dance, to how you manage to stay abreast of being able to produce these things technologically, do you find that amongst all of these concerns that it's hard to position which are the most important concerns – because there's so many, do you find that difficult?

BM   Not really. [laughter]

RB   I don't know I mean we collaborate with often lots of people and sometimes not, sometimes just the two of us. And now I really don't know what a tool is actually. So thanks for that. [laughter] I really don't know what a tool is because, you know – with the different software, coders, coders who think their code is poetry, and all the different people that we work with all bring their stories and they all bring their skills and they all bring their tools.

AM   Do you think a skill is attributed to a tool? So like the form of a particular tool might influence the way that you'd use it and possibly the best way of not using a tool is not being very good at using it.

FN   Maybe it's a fluid process between a tool being developed and people using it. And then that gets fed back in.

AM   Yeah like what came first the job or the tool?

AM   They're made for the job.

CL   There's a really interesting book by Richard Sennett, it's called *The*

Craftsman, in it Sennett makes the connection between weaving and the dove tail joint. He says that the dove tail joint came after weaving. But he said that it also coincided with the Greeks sailing their ships over further distances and the traditional joints started to come undone on the ships. So the coming together of this need for the boats to be sturdier and also a new kind of conception of putting things together in a way that held them stronger – he says that these are the moments when we invent tools.

RZ   I had a question following on from that, between Neil and Colm, the way you describe the Proto-tool and it sounds like it's almost like the conditions which enable you to make a piece of work and the structures that need to be in place – or that being one type of Proto-tool. And this maybe being about the fact that this event is taking place within the context of the publication of the E:vent archive, but also with your work on display Colm and then maybe this is a way of you (Colm) to talk about your practice? Are we your tools? Is this what Proto-tools is? Creating the conditions to enable you to be an artist or something?

CL   Well I think we're all talking about our practice, which is the point – but I suppose maybe when artists get involved in organising art events like this and include themselves in the programme it's always possible to ask this question. I don't know, perhaps there are certain aspects of this event that are unresolved. I think Antonia described the exhibition part as 'kind of an exhibition' to begin with. So we began to talk about it as a *display* rather than an exhibition – and other things happened where one of the artists had to suddenly drop out because of an accident – –

RZ   Surely then it's a very effective demonstration of a misuse of a tool. You've completely screwed up the exhibition, it's unresolved, someone's dropped out, someone's had a motorbike accident – but also, if this is talking about the conditions to create work – or what tools need to be in place, how do you think of this?

CL   I think maybe your question is about the programme of the art object and when and where and how a thing can start to operate as an object of art? For example the work I've put on the walls here, if it's operating as art it's maybe just about, it's very much a scientific image. And it's literally – just to explain what that image is, it's an SEM scan of the wall. I took a small chip from the wall next to where the image is and I took it to Bath University and I got them to do an SEM scan which blows it up 15,000 times. That's what that image is. And also Jonathan's performance was going to use soil from outside in the garden here. So the exhibition part is very much bringing the building itself, Flat Time House, the institution and the process of exhibiting into this question of the extended programme of the art object, from the tool and making to the display. With my work I generally think in terms of programmes, whether things *work* or they get 'screwed up' as you say, doesn't always matter so much to me.

RG   Is everybody here a maker?

AM   How do you define maker?

RG   I'm just wondering – like just then Colm's explanation: 'this is how I did this...'

FN   I think making the process open in some way or playing with how it can be made open however that might be, is interesting – –

AM   Often the process to a piece can be what the piece is about. Whereas sometimes when the piece is about the finished product it's like the magician giving away his tricks, which demystifies it, and it becomes less spectacular. But there are always things where the process makes up for the concept behind making it. So I guess it's what you want the work to say about itself. Whether or not you want the process to be visible or not.

AM   I was going to ask whether we would consider language as a tool?

FN   I was thinking a lot about this. I'm not sure. I like thinking about whether it is or not. Going back to – we were talking about whether there is a binary between traditional tools and contemporary conceptions of what a tool is. And language is something that kind of – –

AM   I was thinking that when the first tools came and man is looking for things that fit to his hand I guess that maybe it's the same with language – to try and find things that fit with social prognitions possibly. And these are tools that don't need to exist on a physical plane simply because we're not using them in a physical manner. But there is no language part of the brain, it's a very – it's a cultural development. And also you can misuse language as well. So I guess maybe we can begin to see language as a tool. I could start talking nonsense and misusing it. And there is a particular skill as well, I find, involved with language.

FN   I was thinking about the difference between language and meaning in relationship to using it and producing it. Is it a mediator between us all now or is it something that we're making through speaking it? I don't know – I'm going off now into some territory I think.

AM   I just wanted to say something in terms of defining the tool. Because we are using hundreds of things in order to make something but I think to identify what *the* tool was to make something is to identify what we made. So there is a connection – I mean I'm Greek and the Greek word for tool is *ergaleio* which comes from *ergo* which means *work*. So it's important to define what exactly was the work you did with the tool in order to know what, from the millions of things used, was your tool for this work. Because yes you might use language or nails, or paint but your tools might be a person as we said yesterday.

CL   I was talking to a friend about Proto-tools and she was making the point that Cornelia Parker's artwork, *Thirty Pieces of Silver* – which was made by laying hundreds of pieces of silverware along a road and driving a steamroller over them – that although when Parker exhibits this work she presents the flattened pieces of silverware suspended from the ceiling, perhaps the *energy* of this work is actually located at the point when the steamroller rolls over the silverware. I think this question, the question of the energy of the work and where and when and what the work starts to pivot around, is an interesting question. And it also seems to related to what Maria is talking about, the steamroller in this case is perhaps the tool, of the many different tools used, this is *the* tool of this work. Perhaps this is the Proto-tool.

AB   I'm going to stop you all there because its five past 5.

COLOPHON

Proto-tools Transcription 1, 16-17 Nov 2013 Flat Time House

Published, London 2014 by Event Media Projects

Edited and designed by Colm Lally

ISBN 978-0-9576627-1-1

Event Media Projects Ltd.
96 Teesdale Street
London, E2 6PU
United Kingdom

www.eventnetwork.org.uk

ACKNOWLEDGMENTS

Proto-tools emerged from conversations between Colm Lally and Antonia Blocker, Neil Chapman and Peter Lewis.

Many thanks to the participants: Antonia Blocker, Neil Chapman, Peter Fillingham, Verina Gfader, Julika Gittner, Mark Harris, Jonathan Kemp, Stephen Knott, Colm Lally, John Latham, Peter Lewis, Gibson/Martelli, Fay Nicolson, Andrés Montenegro Rosero, Alex Schady and Rehana Zaman.

Thanks also to Flat Time House for hosting this 2-day event.

Thanks to Fani Louisa Parali and Mark Harris for help with documentation.

And thanks also to Neil Chapman, Verina Gfader, Julika Gittner, Colm Lally, Gibson/Martelli, Fay Nicolson, Alex Schady and Rehana Zaman for help with proofreading.

www.ingramcontent.com/pod-product-compliance
Lightning Source LLC
Chambersburg PA
CBHW030851180526
45163CB00004B/1532